50 Nourishing Noodles from Asia
Recipes for Home

By: Kelly Johnson

Table of Contents

- Pad Thai
- Ramen
- Pho
- Singapore Noodles
- Yakisoba
- Tom Yum Noodle Soup
- Mee Goreng
- Udon Stir-Fry
- Pad See Ew
- Soba Noodle Salad
- Sesame Garlic Noodles
- Spicy Korean Ramen
- Malaysian Laksa
- Cantonese Chow Mein
- Thai Peanut Noodles
- Vietnamese Egg Noodle Soup
- Japchae (Korean Glass Noodles)
- Curry Mee
- Shrimp Pad Thai
- Kimchi Ramen
- Beef Pho
- Thai Basil Chicken Noodles
- Cold Sesame Noodles
- Miso Ramen
- Chicken Yakitori Udon
- Dan Dan Noodles
- Teriyaki Noodle Stir-Fry
- Szechuan Spicy Noodles
- Indonesian Bakmi Goreng
- Thai Drunken Noodles
- Tempura Soba
- Beef and Broccoli Noodles
- Hainanese Chicken Rice Noodles
- Bibimbap Noodles
- Burmese Coconut Noodle Soup

- Kimchi Udon
- Satay Chicken Noodles
- Hot and Sour Glass Noodle Soup
- Japanese Curry Udon
- Vietnamese Bun Thit Nuong
- Ginger Scallion Noodles
- Teriyaki Chicken Ramen
- Pineapple Fried Rice Noodles
- Thai Red Curry Noodles
- Beef Bulgogi Udon
- Cold Kimchi Noodles
- Japanese Shrimp Tempura Udon
- Pad Kra Pao
- Taiwanese Beef Noodle Soup
- Spicy Sesame Cold Noodles

Pad Thai

Ingredients:

For the Pad Thai Sauce:

- 3 tablespoons tamarind paste
- 3 tablespoons fish sauce (or soy sauce for a vegetarian version)
- 2 tablespoons sugar
- 1 tablespoon rice vinegar
- 1 teaspoon chili sauce (adjust to taste)

For the Pad Thai:

- 8 oz rice noodles, soaked in warm water until softened and drained
- 2 tablespoons vegetable oil
- 1 cup firm tofu, pressed and cubed
- 2 cloves garlic, minced
- 2 eggs (optional for non-vegetarian version)
- 1 cup bean sprouts
- 1 cup shredded carrots
- 4 green onions, sliced
- 1/2 cup chopped peanuts
- Lime wedges for serving

Instructions:

1. Prepare the Pad Thai Sauce:

- In a bowl, whisk together tamarind paste, fish sauce (or soy sauce), sugar, rice vinegar, and chili sauce. Set aside.

2. Cook the Rice Noodles:

- Soak the rice noodles in warm water according to package instructions until they are softened. Drain and set aside.

3. Cook the Tofu:

- In a large wok or skillet, heat 1 tablespoon of vegetable oil over medium-high heat. Add the cubed tofu and cook until golden brown on all sides. Remove from the wok and set aside.

4. Cook the Vegetables:

- In the same wok, add another tablespoon of oil. Add minced garlic and sauté for about 30 seconds. If using eggs, push the garlic to one side of the wok and scramble the eggs on the other side until just cooked.
- Add bean sprouts, shredded carrots, and sliced green onions. Stir-fry for 1-2 minutes until the vegetables are slightly tender.

5. Combine Ingredients:

- Push the vegetables to one side of the wok and add the soaked rice noodles. Pour the prepared Pad Thai sauce over the noodles and toss everything together.

6. Add Tofu and Peanuts:

- Add the cooked tofu back into the wok and toss to combine. Add chopped peanuts and continue to stir-fry for another minute.

7. Serve:

- Divide the Pad Thai among serving plates. Garnish with additional peanuts, bean sprouts, and lime wedges.

Enjoy your homemade Pad Thai! Adjust the spice level and ingredients according to your taste preferences.

Ramen

Ingredients:

For the Broth:

- 4 cups chicken or vegetable broth
- 2 cloves garlic, minced
- 1 tablespoon ginger, grated
- 2 tablespoons soy sauce
- 1 tablespoon mirin
- 1 tablespoon sesame oil

For the Ramen:

- 8 oz ramen noodles
- 2 cups sliced vegetables (e.g., mushrooms, bok choy, carrots, and green onions)
- 2 cups cooked protein (e.g., sliced cooked chicken, pork, tofu, or a soft-boiled egg)

Optional Toppings:

- Nori (seaweed) sheets, sliced
- Sesame seeds
- Red chili flakes
- Sliced green onions
- Lime wedges

Instructions:

1. Prepare the Broth:

- In a large pot, heat sesame oil over medium heat. Add minced garlic and grated ginger, sautéing for about 1 minute until fragrant.
- Pour in the chicken or vegetable broth, soy sauce, and mirin. Bring the broth to a simmer, then reduce the heat and let it simmer for at least 15-20 minutes to allow the flavors to meld.

2. Cook the Ramen Noodles:

- Cook the ramen noodles according to the package instructions. Drain and set aside.

3. Prepare the Toppings:

- While the broth is simmering and the noodles are cooking, prepare your choice of toppings and protein.

4. Assemble the Ramen:

- Divide the cooked ramen noodles among serving bowls.
- Ladle the hot broth over the noodles.
- Arrange the sliced vegetables and protein on top of the noodles.

5. Serve:

- Garnish the ramen with optional toppings such as nori sheets, sesame seeds, red chili flakes, and sliced green onions.
- Serve immediately and enjoy your homemade ramen!

Feel free to customize your ramen by adding your favorite ingredients or adjusting the broth's seasoning to your taste. This basic recipe provides a great starting point for creating your personalized bowl of delicious ramen.

Pho

Ingredients:

For the Broth:

- 1 large onion, halved (unpeeled)
- 1 piece of ginger (about 3 inches), sliced
- 3-4 lbs beef bones (mix of marrow and knuckle bones)
- 1-2 lbs beef brisket or flank
- 3-4 star anise
- 3-4 whole cloves
- 1 cinnamon stick
- 1 cardamom pod
- 1 tablespoon coriander seeds
- 1 tablespoon salt
- 1-2 tablespoons fish sauce
- 1-2 tablespoons soy sauce
- 1-2 tablespoons sugar
- Water (enough to cover the bones)

For the Bowls:

- Rice noodles, cooked according to package instructions
- Thinly sliced beef (from the brisket or flank)
- Bean sprouts
- Fresh basil leaves
- Lime wedges
- Fresh cilantro leaves
- Sliced green onions
- Hoisin sauce and Sriracha for serving

Instructions:

1. Char the Onion and Ginger:

- Preheat your oven broiler. Place the halved onion and sliced ginger on a baking sheet. Broil for about 15-20 minutes until they are nicely charred. Turn them occasionally.

2. Prepare the Broth:

- In a large pot, bring water to a boil. Add the beef bones and boil vigorously for 10 minutes. Discard the water and rinse the bones.
- Fill the pot with fresh water and add the charred onion, ginger, beef brisket or flank, star anise, cloves, cinnamon stick, cardamom pod, coriander seeds, salt, fish sauce, soy sauce, and sugar.
- Bring the pot to a gentle simmer. Skim off any impurities that rise to the surface.
- Simmer the broth for at least 1.5 to 2 hours. The longer it simmers, the richer the flavor.

3. Prepare the Bowls:

- Cook the rice noodles according to the package instructions.
- Thinly slice the cooked beef brisket or flank.
- Arrange the cooked noodles, sliced beef, and desired toppings (bean sprouts, basil, lime wedges, cilantro, and green onions) in serving bowls.

4. Serve:

- Pour the hot broth over the noodles and beef slices.
- Allow diners to customize their bowls with the fresh toppings.
- Serve immediately with hoisin sauce and Sriracha on the side.

Enjoy your homemade Pho! Adjust the seasonings and toppings to suit your taste preferences.

Singapore Noodles

Ingredients:

For the Noodles:

- 8 oz thin rice vermicelli noodles
- 2 tablespoons vegetable oil
- 2 cloves garlic, minced
- 1 tablespoon ginger, grated
- 1 onion, thinly sliced
- 1 bell pepper, thinly sliced
- 1 carrot, julienned
- 1 cup cabbage, thinly sliced
- 1 cup bean sprouts
- 2 green onions, sliced
- 2 eggs, lightly beaten
- 1/2 cup cooked and shredded chicken (optional)
- 1/2 cup cooked shrimp, peeled and deveined (optional)
- 2 tablespoons curry powder
- 1-2 tablespoons soy sauce
- 1 tablespoon oyster sauce
- Salt and pepper to taste
- Lime wedges for serving

Instructions:

Prepare the Rice Vermicelli:
- Cook the rice vermicelli noodles according to the package instructions. Usually, you need to soak them in hot water for about 5-7 minutes until they are soft but still have a bit of bite. Drain and set aside.

Stir-Fry Vegetables:
- Heat vegetable oil in a wok or large skillet over medium-high heat. Add minced garlic and grated ginger, stir-frying for about 30 seconds until fragrant.
- Add sliced onions, bell pepper, julienned carrot, and sliced cabbage. Stir-fry for 2-3 minutes until the vegetables are slightly softened.

- Push the vegetables to the side of the wok, add a bit more oil if needed, and pour the beaten eggs into the empty space. Scramble the eggs until cooked through.

Combine Ingredients:
- Mix the scrambled eggs with the vegetables. Add cooked and shredded chicken or shrimp if using.
- Add the cooked rice vermicelli noodles to the wok.

Season and Toss:
- Sprinkle curry powder over the ingredients and add soy sauce and oyster sauce. Toss everything together until well combined.
- Season with salt and pepper to taste. Adjust the seasoning if needed.

Finish and Serve:
- Add bean sprouts and sliced green onions to the wok. Toss briefly to incorporate.
- Serve the Singapore noodles hot, garnished with additional green onions and lime wedges on the side.

Enjoy your homemade Singapore Noodles! Feel free to customize the protein and vegetables based on your preferences.

Yakisoba

Ingredients:

For the Yakisoba Sauce:

- 3 tablespoons soy sauce
- 2 tablespoons Worcestershire sauce
- 1 tablespoon oyster sauce
- 1 tablespoon ketchup
- 1 tablespoon sugar

For the Yakisoba:

- 8 oz Yakisoba noodles (or substitute with ramen or Chinese egg noodles)
- 2 tablespoons vegetable oil
- 1 onion, thinly sliced
- 2 carrots, julienned
- 1 bell pepper, thinly sliced
- 2 cups shredded cabbage
- 1 cup bean sprouts
- 2 cloves garlic, minced
- 1 cup sliced cooked protein (chicken, pork, shrimp, or tofu)
- Salt and pepper to taste
- Green onions, chopped (for garnish)
- Pickled ginger (optional, for serving)

Instructions:

For the Yakisoba Sauce:

In a small bowl, whisk together soy sauce, Worcestershire sauce, oyster sauce, ketchup, and sugar. Set aside.

For the Yakisoba:

Cook the Yakisoba noodles according to the package instructions. Drain and set aside.

In a large wok or skillet, heat vegetable oil over medium-high heat.

Add sliced onions, julienned carrots, and sliced bell pepper. Stir-fry for 2-3 minutes until the vegetables start to soften.

Add minced garlic and continue to stir-fry for an additional 30 seconds until fragrant.

Push the vegetables to one side of the wok and add the sliced cooked protein to the other side. Cook briefly until heated through.

Add the shredded cabbage and bean sprouts to the wok. Stir-fry for another 2-3 minutes until the cabbage is wilted.

Add the cooked Yakisoba noodles to the wok, breaking them apart with chopsticks or tongs.

Pour the Yakisoba sauce over the noodles and toss everything together until well coated and heated through.

Season with salt and pepper to taste.

Garnish with chopped green onions.

Serve the Yakisoba hot, with optional pickled ginger on the side.

Enjoy your homemade Yakisoba! This versatile dish can be customized with your favorite vegetables and protein choices.

Tom Yum Noodle Soup

Ingredients:

For the Broth:

- 4 cups chicken or vegetable broth
- 2 stalks lemongrass, smashed and cut into 2-inch pieces
- 3-4 kaffir lime leaves
- 1-2 red bird's eye chilies, smashed (adjust to taste)
- 3 tablespoons fish sauce
- 1 tablespoon soy sauce
- 1 tablespoon tom yum paste (optional for extra flavor)
- 1 tablespoon tamarind paste
- 1 tablespoon brown sugar
- 1-inch piece galangal or ginger, sliced
- 3 cloves garlic, minced

For the Noodle Soup:

- 8 oz rice noodles, cooked according to package instructions
- 1 cup sliced mushrooms (such as button or shiitake)
- 1 medium tomato, cut into wedges
- 1/2 cup tofu, diced (optional)
- 1 cup baby bok choy or spinach, chopped
- Fresh cilantro leaves for garnish
- Lime wedges for serving

Instructions:

1. Prepare the Broth:

- In a pot, bring the chicken or vegetable broth to a simmer over medium heat.
- Add lemongrass, kaffir lime leaves, red chilies, fish sauce, soy sauce, tom yum paste (if using), tamarind paste, brown sugar, galangal or ginger, and minced garlic. Simmer for about 10-15 minutes to infuse the flavors.

2. Cook the Noodles:

- Cook the rice noodles according to the package instructions. Drain and set aside.

3. Assemble the Noodle Soup:

- Strain the broth to remove the lemongrass, kaffir lime leaves, and galangal or ginger slices.
- Return the strained broth to the pot and bring it back to a simmer.
- Add sliced mushrooms, tomato wedges, diced tofu (if using), and baby bok choy or spinach. Cook for 3-5 minutes until the vegetables are tender.
- Add the cooked rice noodles to the pot and stir to combine.

4. Serve:

- Ladle the Tom Yum Noodle Soup into serving bowls.
- Garnish with fresh cilantro leaves.
- Serve with lime wedges on the side for squeezing.

Enjoy your homemade Tom Yum Noodle Soup! Adjust the level of spiciness and other seasonings according to your taste preferences.

Mee Goreng

Ingredients:

For the Sauce:

- 3 tablespoons soy sauce
- 2 tablespoons kecap manis (sweet soy sauce)
- 1 tablespoon oyster sauce
- 1 tablespoon tomato ketchup
- 1 tablespoon fish sauce
- 1 tablespoon lime juice
- 1 teaspoon brown sugar

For the Noodles:

- 8 oz egg noodles or yellow noodles, cooked according to package instructions and drained
- 2 tablespoons vegetable oil
- 2 cloves garlic, minced
- 1 small onion, sliced
- 1 red chili, sliced (adjust to taste)
- 1 cup cabbage, shredded
- 1 carrot, julienned
- 1 bell pepper, sliced
- 1 cup bean sprouts
- 2 eggs, lightly beaten
- Green onions, chopped (for garnish)
- Fried shallots (optional, for garnish)
- Lime wedges (for serving)

Instructions:

1. Prepare the Sauce:

- In a small bowl, mix together soy sauce, kecap manis, oyster sauce, tomato ketchup, fish sauce, lime juice, and brown sugar. Set aside.

2. Cook the Noodles:

- Cook the egg noodles or yellow noodles according to the package instructions. Drain and set aside.

3. Stir-Fry:

- Heat vegetable oil in a wok or large skillet over medium-high heat.
- Add minced garlic and sliced onion. Stir-fry for about 1-2 minutes until fragrant and the onion is softened.
- Add the red chili, shredded cabbage, julienned carrot, and sliced bell pepper. Stir-fry for another 2-3 minutes until the vegetables are slightly tender.
- Push the vegetables to the side of the wok and pour the beaten eggs into the empty space. Scramble the eggs until just cooked.

4. Combine and Sauce:

- Add the cooked and drained noodles to the wok. Pour the prepared sauce over the noodles and toss everything together until well coated.
- Add bean sprouts and continue to stir-fry for an additional 2-3 minutes until the noodles are heated through and the bean sprouts are slightly cooked.

5. Garnish and Serve:

- Garnish the Mee Goreng with chopped green onions and, if desired, fried shallots.
- Serve hot with lime wedges on the side.

Enjoy your homemade Mee Goreng! Adjust the spice level and ingredients according to your taste preferences.

Udon Stir-Fry

Ingredients:

For the Stir-Fry Sauce:

- 3 tablespoons soy sauce
- 2 tablespoons oyster sauce
- 1 tablespoon mirin
- 1 tablespoon sake (optional)
- 1 tablespoon brown sugar
- 1 teaspoon sesame oil

For the Udon Stir-Fry:

- 8 oz udon noodles, cooked according to package instructions and drained
- 2 tablespoons vegetable oil
- 2 cloves garlic, minced
- 1 tablespoon fresh ginger, grated
- 1 carrot, julienned
- 1 bell pepper, thinly sliced
- 1 cup broccoli florets
- 1 cup snap peas, ends trimmed
- 1 cup sliced mushrooms
- 1 cup firm tofu or protein of choice, diced
- Green onions, sliced (for garnish)
- Sesame seeds (for garnish)

Instructions:

1. Prepare the Stir-Fry Sauce:

- In a small bowl, whisk together soy sauce, oyster sauce, mirin, sake (if using), brown sugar, and sesame oil. Set aside.

2. Cook the Udon Noodles:

- Cook the udon noodles according to the package instructions. Drain and set aside.

3. Stir-Fry:

- Heat vegetable oil in a wok or large skillet over medium-high heat.
- Add minced garlic and grated ginger. Stir-fry for about 30 seconds until fragrant.
- Add julienned carrot, sliced bell pepper, broccoli florets, snap peas, sliced mushrooms, and diced tofu (or protein of choice). Stir-fry for 3-5 minutes until the vegetables are slightly tender and the tofu is cooked through.

4. Combine and Sauce:

- Add the cooked udon noodles to the wok.
- Pour the prepared stir-fry sauce over the noodles and vegetables. Toss everything together until well coated.

5. Garnish and Serve:

- Garnish the Udon Stir-Fry with sliced green onions and sesame seeds.
- Serve hot and enjoy your delicious Udon Stir-Fry!

Feel free to customize the vegetables and protein based on your preferences. This versatile dish is quick to make and packed with savory flavors.

Pad See Ew

Ingredients:

For the Sauce:

- 3 tablespoons soy sauce
- 2 tablespoons oyster sauce
- 1 tablespoon dark soy sauce (for color)
- 1 tablespoon fish sauce
- 1 tablespoon sugar
- 1/2 teaspoon white pepper

For the Pad See Ew:

- 8 oz wide rice noodles, fresh or soaked according to package instructions
- 2 tablespoons vegetable oil
- 2 cloves garlic, minced
- 1 cup Chinese broccoli or broccoli florets, chopped
- 1 cup thinly sliced protein (chicken, beef, or tofu)
- 2 large eggs, lightly beaten

Instructions:

1. Prepare the Sauce:

- In a small bowl, whisk together soy sauce, oyster sauce, dark soy sauce, fish sauce, sugar, and white pepper. Set aside.

2. Cook the Rice Noodles:

- If using fresh rice noodles, blanch them briefly in hot water to loosen them. If using dried noodles, soak them according to the package instructions. Drain and set aside.

3. Stir-Fry:

- Heat vegetable oil in a wok or large skillet over medium-high heat.
- Add minced garlic and stir-fry for about 30 seconds until fragrant.
- Add the sliced protein (chicken, beef, or tofu) and cook until browned and cooked through.
- Push the protein to one side of the wok and pour the beaten eggs into the empty space. Scramble the eggs until just cooked.
- Add the chopped Chinese broccoli or broccoli to the wok and stir-fry for a couple of minutes until the vegetables are tender-crisp.

4. Combine and Sauce:

- Add the cooked rice noodles to the wok.
- Pour the prepared sauce over the noodles and toss everything together until well combined and heated through.

5. Serve:

- Serve the Pad See Ew hot, garnished with additional white pepper if desired.

Enjoy your homemade Pad See Ew! Feel free to customize the protein and vegetables based on your preferences.

Soba Noodle Salad

Ingredients:

For the Dressing:

- 3 tablespoons soy sauce
- 2 tablespoons rice vinegar
- 1 tablespoon sesame oil
- 1 tablespoon honey or maple syrup
- 1 teaspoon grated ginger
- 1 teaspoon minced garlic
- 1 tablespoon sesame seeds (optional)
- Crushed red pepper flakes, to taste (optional)

For the Salad:

- 8 oz soba noodles
- 1 cup shredded carrots
- 1 cucumber, julienned
- 1 bell pepper (red, yellow, or orange), thinly sliced
- 1 cup shredded red cabbage
- 1/2 cup chopped scallions (green onions)
- 1/4 cup chopped cilantro
- 1/4 cup chopped mint
- 1/4 cup chopped roasted peanuts or cashews (optional)

Instructions:

1. Prepare the Dressing:

- In a small bowl, whisk together soy sauce, rice vinegar, sesame oil, honey or maple syrup, grated ginger, minced garlic, sesame seeds (if using), and crushed red pepper flakes (if using). Set aside.

2. Cook the Soba Noodles:

- Cook the soba noodles according to the package instructions. Drain and rinse them under cold water to stop the cooking process. Allow them to cool.

3. Assemble the Salad:

- In a large mixing bowl, combine the cooled soba noodles, shredded carrots, julienned cucumber, sliced bell pepper, shredded red cabbage, chopped scallions, chopped cilantro, and chopped mint.
- Pour the dressing over the salad and toss everything together until well coated.

4. Serve:

- Garnish the Soba Noodle Salad with chopped roasted peanuts or cashews (if using).
- Serve chilled and enjoy!

This Soba Noodle Salad is not only flavorful but also versatile. You can customize it by adding your favorite protein, such as grilled chicken, shrimp, or tofu. It's a perfect dish for a refreshing lunch or light dinner.

Sesame Garlic Noodles

Ingredients:

For the Sauce:

- 1/4 cup soy sauce
- 2 tablespoons sesame oil
- 1 tablespoon rice vinegar
- 1 tablespoon honey or maple syrup
- 2 cloves garlic, minced
- 1 tablespoon grated fresh ginger
- 1 tablespoon tahini (optional)
- 1 teaspoon chili oil or Sriracha sauce (adjust to taste)

For the Noodles:

- 8 oz Asian wheat noodles or linguine
- 2 tablespoons vegetable oil
- 1 bell pepper, thinly sliced
- 1 carrot, julienned
- 1 cup broccoli florets
- 1/4 cup chopped green onions (for garnish)
- 1 tablespoon sesame seeds (for garnish)
- Lime wedges (for serving)

Instructions:

1. Prepare the Sauce:

- In a bowl, whisk together soy sauce, sesame oil, rice vinegar, honey or maple syrup, minced garlic, grated ginger, tahini (if using), and chili oil or Sriracha. Set aside.

2. Cook the Noodles:

- Cook the Asian wheat noodles or linguine according to the package instructions. Drain and set aside.

3. Stir-Fry:

- In a large skillet or wok, heat vegetable oil over medium-high heat.
- Add sliced bell pepper, julienned carrot, and broccoli florets. Stir-fry for 3-4 minutes until the vegetables are tender-crisp.

4. Combine and Toss:

- Add the cooked noodles to the skillet or wok.
- Pour the prepared sauce over the noodles and vegetables.
- Toss everything together until the noodles and vegetables are well coated with the sauce.

5. Garnish and Serve:

- Garnish the Sesame Garlic Noodles with chopped green onions and sesame seeds.
- Serve hot, and squeeze lime wedges over the noodles before eating, if desired.

Enjoy your delicious Sesame Garlic Noodles! This dish is versatile, and you can add your favorite proteins such as grilled chicken, shrimp, or tofu for a more substantial meal.

Spicy Korean Ramen

Ingredients:

For the Broth:

- 4 cups chicken or vegetable broth
- 2 cloves garlic, minced
- 1 tablespoon ginger, grated
- 2 tablespoons gochujang (Korean red chili paste)
- 1 tablespoon soy sauce
- 1 tablespoon sesame oil
- 1 tablespoon brown sugar
- 1 tablespoon rice vinegar
- 1 teaspoon gochugaru (Korean red pepper flakes, adjust to taste)

For the Ramen:

- 2 packs of Korean instant ramen noodles (Shin Ramyun or your preferred brand)
- 1 cup sliced mushrooms
- 1 cup baby spinach or bok choy, chopped
- 1 cup shredded carrots
- 2 green onions, sliced
- 2 boiled eggs, halved (optional)
- Sesame seeds and nori (seaweed) for garnish

Instructions:

1. Prepare the Broth:

- In a pot, combine chicken or vegetable broth, minced garlic, grated ginger, gochujang, soy sauce, sesame oil, brown sugar, rice vinegar, and gochugaru. Bring the mixture to a simmer over medium heat and let it simmer for about 10-15 minutes to allow the flavors to meld.

2. Cook the Ramen:

- Cook the Korean instant ramen noodles according to the package instructions. Drain and set aside.

3. Assemble the Ramen:

- Divide the cooked noodles among serving bowls.
- Pour the hot spicy broth over the noodles.
- Add sliced mushrooms, shredded carrots, chopped spinach or bok choy, and green onions to each bowl.
- Garnish with boiled egg halves, sesame seeds, and torn nori sheets.

4. Serve:

- Serve the Spicy Korean Ramen hot, and enjoy the bold flavors!

Feel free to customize this recipe by adding your favorite protein, such as sliced beef, chicken, or tofu. Adjust the spiciness level according to your taste preference by varying the amount of gochugaru and gochujang.

Malaysian Laksa

Ingredients:

For the Laksa Paste:

- 3 stalks lemongrass, chopped
- 4 shallots, peeled and chopped
- 4 cloves garlic, peeled
- 1 thumb-sized piece of galangal, sliced
- 1 thumb-sized piece of ginger, sliced
- 4 dried red chilies, soaked in hot water
- 1 tablespoon coriander powder
- 1 teaspoon turmeric powder
- 2 tablespoons shrimp paste (belacan)
- 2 tablespoons vegetable oil

For the Laksa Broth:

- 2 tablespoons vegetable oil
- 400 ml coconut milk
- 1 liter chicken or vegetable broth
- 1 tablespoon tamarind paste
- 2 tablespoons fish sauce
- 1 tablespoon soy sauce
- 1 tablespoon palm sugar or brown sugar
- Salt to taste

For the Laksa Toppings:

- Rice vermicelli or thick rice noodles, cooked according to package instructions
- Cooked chicken, prawns, or tofu
- Bean sprouts
- Hard-boiled eggs, halved
- Fresh cilantro leaves
- Lime wedges

Instructions:

1. Prepare the Laksa Paste:

    In a food processor, blend lemongrass, shallots, garlic, galangal, ginger, soaked dried chilies, coriander powder, turmeric powder, and shrimp paste until a smooth paste forms.
    Heat 2 tablespoons of vegetable oil in a pan over medium heat. Add the paste and sauté for 5-7 minutes until fragrant.

2. Make the Laksa Broth:

    In a large pot, heat 2 tablespoons of vegetable oil. Add the laksa paste and cook for another 2-3 minutes.
    Pour in the coconut milk, chicken or vegetable broth, tamarind paste, fish sauce, soy sauce, and palm sugar. Bring the mixture to a simmer.
    Allow the broth to simmer for about 15-20 minutes to develop the flavors. Season with salt to taste.

3. Assemble the Laksa:

    Prepare rice vermicelli or thick rice noodles according to the package instructions.
    Divide the cooked noodles among serving bowls and ladle the hot laksa broth over them.
    Add your choice of protein (cooked chicken, prawns, or tofu).
    Top the laksa with bean sprouts, hard-boiled eggs, fresh cilantro leaves, and lime wedges.
    Serve hot and enjoy your Malaysian Laksa!

Feel free to adjust the spiciness and ingredients to suit your taste preferences. Laksa is a versatile dish that can be customized with various proteins and toppings.

Cantonese Chow Mein

Ingredients:

For the Noodles:

- 8 oz Cantonese-style egg noodles or Hong Kong-style pan-fried noodles
- 2 tablespoons vegetable oil

For the Stir-Fry:

- 2 tablespoons vegetable oil
- 2 cloves garlic, minced
- 1 cup sliced shiitake mushrooms (or any preferred mushrooms)
- 1 cup julienned carrots
- 1 cup sliced bell peppers (any color)
- 1 cup sliced Napa cabbage
- 1 cup bean sprouts
- 1 cup sliced green onions (scallions)
- 1/4 cup soy sauce
- 2 tablespoons oyster sauce
- 1 tablespoon cornstarch (mixed with 2 tablespoons water)
- Sesame oil for drizzling (optional)
- Toasted sesame seeds for garnish (optional)

Instructions:

1. Prepare the Noodles:

   Cook the Cantonese-style egg noodles or pan-fried noodles according to the package instructions. Drain and set aside.
   Heat 2 tablespoons of vegetable oil in a large wok or skillet over medium-high heat. Add the cooked noodles and spread them out into an even layer. Allow them to cook undisturbed for 3-5 minutes until the bottom becomes crispy. Flip the noodles over and crisp the other side. Once crispy, transfer the noodles to a serving plate.

2. Stir-Fry:

   In the same wok or skillet, heat 2 tablespoons of vegetable oil over medium-high heat.
   Add minced garlic and stir-fry for about 30 seconds until fragrant.
   Add sliced shiitake mushrooms, julienned carrots, and sliced bell peppers. Stir-fry for 2-3 minutes until the vegetables start to soften.
   Add sliced Napa cabbage, bean sprouts, and sliced green onions. Continue to stir-fry for another 2-3 minutes until the vegetables are tender-crisp.

3. Sauce and Finish:

   In a small bowl, mix soy sauce and oyster sauce together. Pour the sauce over the stir-fried vegetables.
   Pour the cornstarch-water mixture into the wok to thicken the sauce. Stir everything together until well coated.
   Pour the vegetable mixture over the crispy noodles.

4. Serve:

   Drizzle with sesame oil if desired and garnish with toasted sesame seeds.
   Serve the Cantonese Chow Mein hot and enjoy your delicious and crispy noodle stir-fry!

Feel free to customize the vegetables and adjust the sauce to suit your preferences.

Thai Peanut Noodles

Ingredients:

For the Peanut Sauce:

- 1/3 cup creamy peanut butter
- 3 tablespoons soy sauce
- 2 tablespoons honey or maple syrup
- 2 tablespoons rice vinegar
- 1 tablespoon sesame oil
- 1 tablespoon grated ginger
- 2 cloves garlic, minced
- 1 teaspoon Sriracha or chili garlic sauce (adjust to taste)
- 2-4 tablespoons water (to thin the sauce)

For the Noodles:

- 8 oz rice noodles or linguine
- 2 tablespoons vegetable oil
- 1 red bell pepper, thinly sliced
- 1 carrot, julienned or grated
- 1 cucumber, julienned or spiralized
- 1 cup shredded purple cabbage
- 1/4 cup chopped peanuts (for garnish)
- Fresh cilantro and lime wedges (for garnish)

Instructions:

1. Prepare the Peanut Sauce:

   In a bowl, whisk together peanut butter, soy sauce, honey or maple syrup, rice vinegar, sesame oil, grated ginger, minced garlic, and Sriracha or chili garlic sauce until smooth.
   If the sauce is too thick, add 2-4 tablespoons of water to achieve the desired consistency. Set aside.

2. Cook the Noodles:

   Cook the rice noodles or linguine according to the package instructions. Drain and rinse under cold water to stop the cooking process. Toss the noodles with a bit of oil to prevent sticking.

3. Stir-Fry:

   In a large skillet or wok, heat vegetable oil over medium-high heat.
   Add sliced red bell pepper, julienned carrot, and shredded purple cabbage. Stir-fry for 3-5 minutes until the vegetables are slightly softened but still crisp.
   Add the cooked and drained noodles to the skillet. Pour the peanut sauce over the noodles and vegetables.
   Toss everything together until well coated and heated through.

4. Garnish and Serve:

   Garnish the Thai Peanut Noodles with chopped peanuts, fresh cilantro, and lime wedges.
   Serve hot or cold, and enjoy your delicious Thai Peanut Noodles!

Feel free to customize the recipe by adding protein of your choice, such as grilled chicken, shrimp, or tofu. Adjust the spice level and other ingredients based on your preferences.

Vietnamese Egg Noodle Soup

Ingredients:

For the Broth:

- 1 whole chicken (about 3-4 pounds)
- 1 onion, halved
- 2-3 inches ginger, sliced
- 2-3 cloves garlic, crushed
- 1 tablespoon salt
- 1 tablespoon fish sauce
- 1 tablespoon sugar
- 1 teaspoon black peppercorns

For the Noodle Soup:

- 8 oz egg noodles (miến or thin egg noodles)
- 1 cup bean sprouts, rinsed
- Fresh cilantro, chopped
- Green onions, sliced
- Fresh lime wedges

Optional Garnishes:

- Red chili slices
- Fresh basil leaves
- Mint leaves

Instructions:

1. Prepare the Chicken Broth:

   Clean the chicken and remove any excess fat. Rinse it under cold water.
   In a large pot, bring about 4 quarts of water to a boil. Add the whole chicken, onion halves, ginger slices, crushed garlic, salt, fish sauce, sugar, and black peppercorns.

Reduce the heat to low and let it simmer for about 1.5 to 2 hours, skimming off any impurities that rise to the surface.

Once the chicken is cooked through and the broth is flavorful, remove the chicken from the pot. Allow it to cool, then shred the meat.

Strain the broth through a fine-mesh sieve or cheesecloth to achieve a clear broth. Adjust the seasoning with more salt, fish sauce, or sugar if needed.

2. Cook the Egg Noodles:

Cook the egg noodles according to the package instructions. Drain and rinse under cold water to stop the cooking process.

3. Assemble the Vietnamese Egg Noodle Soup:

In serving bowls, place a portion of cooked egg noodles.
Top the noodles with shredded chicken.
Ladle the hot chicken broth over the noodles and chicken.
Garnish with bean sprouts, chopped cilantro, and sliced green onions.

4. Serve:

Serve the Vietnamese Egg Noodle Soup hot.
Offer lime wedges and optional garnishes like red chili slices, fresh basil leaves, and mint leaves on the side.

Enjoy your comforting and flavorful Vietnamese Egg Noodle Soup! Feel free to adjust the garnishes and seasonings according to your taste preferences.

Japchae (Korean Glass Noodles)

Ingredients:

For the Glass Noodles:

- 6 oz Korean sweet potato starch noodles (dangmyeon)
- 2 tablespoons sesame oil
- 2 tablespoons soy sauce
- 1 tablespoon sugar
- 1 tablespoon mirin (optional)
- 1 teaspoon minced garlic
- 1 tablespoon vegetable oil (for cooking)

For the Vegetables:

- 1 medium carrot, julienned
- 1 red bell pepper, thinly sliced
- 1 yellow bell pepper, thinly sliced
- 1 onion, thinly sliced
- 2 cups spinach, blanched and squeezed dry
- 4-5 shiitake mushrooms, sliced (or any preferred mushrooms)
- 2 green onions, sliced diagonally (for garnish)

Instructions:

1. Prepare the Glass Noodles:

    Cook the sweet potato starch noodles (dangmyeon) according to the package instructions. Usually, you'll need to soak them in hot water for about 5-7 minutes until they are soft but still have a bit of bite. Drain and set aside.
    In a bowl, mix sesame oil, soy sauce, sugar, mirin (if using), and minced garlic. Toss the cooked noodles in the sauce mixture until well coated. Set aside.

2. Stir-Fry the Vegetables:

    Heat vegetable oil in a large pan or wok over medium-high heat.

Add sliced onions and stir-fry until they become translucent.
Add julienned carrots, sliced bell peppers, and shiitake mushrooms. Stir-fry for about 5 minutes until the vegetables are tender but still slightly crisp.
Add blanched spinach to the pan and toss until combined with the other vegetables.

3. Combine and Finish:

Add the sauced glass noodles to the pan with the vegetables. Toss everything together until well combined.
Adjust the seasoning if needed, adding more soy sauce or sugar according to your taste.

4. Garnish and Serve:

Garnish the Japchae with sliced green onions.
Serve hot or at room temperature.

Enjoy your delicious and colorful Japchae! This dish is often served as a side dish or a main course in Korean cuisine. Feel free to add proteins like beef, chicken, or tofu if you'd like.

Curry Mee

Ingredients:

For the Curry Paste:

- 3 shallots, peeled
- 3 cloves garlic, peeled
- 1 inch ginger, peeled
- 2 tablespoons curry powder
- 1 tablespoon chili paste (adjust to taste)
- 1 tablespoon shrimp paste (belacan), optional
- 1 lemongrass stalk, white part only, sliced

For the Curry Mee:

- 200g (7 oz) rice vermicelli or yellow noodles, cooked according to package instructions
- 200g (7 oz) thick rice noodles (lai fun or laksa noodles), cooked according to package instructions
- 200g (7 oz) chicken, sliced
- 200g (7 oz) prawns, peeled and deveined
- 1 can (400ml) coconut milk
- 4 cups chicken broth
- 2 tablespoons curry powder
- 1 tablespoon chili paste (adjust to taste)
- 2 tablespoons vegetable oil
- 2 tablespoons soy sauce
- 1 tablespoon fish sauce
- 1 tablespoon sugar
- Salt to taste

Toppings and Garnishes:

- Bean sprouts
- Hard-boiled eggs, halved
- Fried tofu puffs, sliced
- Fresh cilantro leaves
- Lime wedges

- Fried shallots

Instructions:

1. Prepare the Curry Paste:

    In a blender or food processor, blend together shallots, garlic, ginger, curry powder, chili paste, shrimp paste (if using), and lemongrass until you get a smooth paste.

2. Cook the Curry Mee:

    In a large pot, heat vegetable oil over medium heat. Add the curry paste and sauté for 2-3 minutes until fragrant.
    Add chicken slices and prawns to the pot. Cook until the chicken is no longer pink and the prawns turn pink.
    Pour in coconut milk and chicken broth. Stir well.
    Add curry powder, chili paste, soy sauce, fish sauce, sugar, and salt. Adjust the seasoning according to your taste.
    Simmer the broth for 10-15 minutes to allow the flavors to meld.

3. Assemble and Serve:

    In serving bowls, place a portion of cooked rice vermicelli, thick rice noodles, chicken, and prawns.
    Ladle the hot curry broth over the noodles and ingredients.
    Top the Curry Mee with bean sprouts, hard-boiled eggs, tofu puffs, fresh cilantro leaves, lime wedges, and fried shallots.
    Serve immediately and enjoy your homemade Curry Mee!

Feel free to customize the toppings and adjust the spiciness according to your preferences. Curry Mee is a comforting and flavorful dish that's perfect for any meal.

Shrimp Pad Thai

Ingredients:

For the Pad Thai Sauce:

- 3 tablespoons tamarind paste
- 2 tablespoons fish sauce
- 1 tablespoon soy sauce
- 1 tablespoon oyster sauce
- 1 tablespoon sugar
- 1/2 teaspoon chili flakes (adjust to taste)

For the Pad Thai:

- 8 oz rice noodles (flat, medium-width)
- 2 tablespoons vegetable oil
- 1 cup shrimp, peeled and deveined
- 2 cloves garlic, minced
- 1 cup firm tofu, diced (optional)
- 2 eggs, lightly beaten
- 1 cup bean sprouts
- 1 cup chives or green onions, chopped
- 1/2 cup roasted peanuts, chopped
- Lime wedges for serving

Instructions:

1. Prepare the Pad Thai Sauce:

    In a bowl, mix together tamarind paste, fish sauce, soy sauce, oyster sauce, sugar, and chili flakes. Stir until the sugar dissolves. Set aside.

2. Cook the Rice Noodles:

    Cook the rice noodles according to the package instructions. Drain and set aside.

3. Stir-Fry:

   Heat vegetable oil in a wok or large skillet over medium-high heat.
   Add minced garlic and cook for about 30 seconds until fragrant.
   Add shrimp to the wok and stir-fry until they turn pink and opaque.
   Push the shrimp to one side of the wok and pour the beaten eggs into the empty space. Scramble the eggs until just cooked.
   Add diced tofu (if using) and cooked rice noodles to the wok.

4. Add Sauce and Toss:

   Pour the prepared Pad Thai sauce over the noodles and ingredients.
   Toss everything together until well combined and heated through.

5. Finish and Garnish:

   Add bean sprouts and chopped chives or green onions to the wok. Toss for an additional minute until the bean sprouts are slightly cooked.
   Remove the wok from heat.

6. Serve:

   Serve Shrimp Pad Thai hot, garnished with chopped roasted peanuts.
   Serve with lime wedges on the side for squeezing over the Pad Thai before eating.

Enjoy your delicious homemade Shrimp Pad Thai! Adjust the spice level and ingredients according to your taste preferences.

Kimchi Ramen

Ingredients:

For the Kimchi Ramen:

- 2 packs of ramen noodles
- 1 cup kimchi, chopped
- 1 cup kimchi juice (from the kimchi jar)
- 4 cups vegetable or chicken broth
- 1 tablespoon soy sauce
- 1 tablespoon gochugaru (Korean red pepper flakes, adjust to taste)
- 1 tablespoon sesame oil
- 1 tablespoon minced garlic
- 1 tablespoon minced ginger
- 2 green onions, sliced (for garnish)
- 2 boiled eggs, halved (optional, for serving)

Instructions:

1. Prepare the Broth:

    In a pot, heat vegetable or chicken broth over medium heat.
    Add chopped kimchi, kimchi juice, soy sauce, gochugaru, minced garlic, and minced ginger to the broth. Stir well.
    Simmer the broth for about 10-15 minutes to allow the flavors to meld.

2. Cook the Ramen Noodles:

    Cook the ramen noodles according to the package instructions. Drain and set aside.

3. Assemble the Kimchi Ramen:

    Divide the cooked ramen noodles among serving bowls.
    Ladle the hot kimchi broth over the noodles.

4. Garnish and Serve:

    Drizzle each bowl with sesame oil.

Garnish with sliced green onions and add a halved boiled egg if desired.
Serve the Kimchi Ramen hot and enjoy!

Feel free to customize this recipe by adding other ingredients like tofu, mushrooms, or spinach. Adjust the spice level according to your taste preference by varying the amount of gochugaru.

Beef Pho

Ingredients:

For the Broth:

- 1 large onion, halved and unpeeled
- 1 4-inch piece of ginger, sliced
- 4-5 lbs beef bones (marrow and knuckle bones)
- 1 lb beef brisket or beef sirloin, thinly sliced
- 3-4 star anise
- 3-4 whole cloves
- 1 cinnamon stick
- 1 cardamom pod
- 1 tablespoon coriander seeds
- 1 tablespoon salt
- 2-3 tablespoons fish sauce
- 1-2 tablespoons sugar
- Water (enough to cover the bones, about 4 quarts)

For Serving:

- Flat rice noodles (banh pho), cooked according to package instructions
- Bean sprouts
- Fresh herbs (cilantro, basil, mint)
- Lime wedges
- Thinly sliced green onions
- Chili slices (optional)
- Hoisin sauce and Sriracha (optional)

Instructions:

1. Prepare the Broth:

    Char the onion and ginger: Place the onion and ginger on a baking sheet and broil in the oven or char over an open flame until they are slightly blackened.

Parboil the bones: Bring a large pot of water to a boil. Add the beef bones and boil vigorously for 10 minutes. Discard the water and rinse the bones with warm water.

Clean the pot: Rinse out the pot to remove any impurities, then return the bones to the pot.

Simmer the broth: Add enough fresh water to the pot to cover the bones (about 4 quarts). Add the charred onion, ginger, star anise, cloves, cinnamon stick, cardamom pod, coriander seeds, salt, fish sauce, and sugar.

Bring to a boil, then reduce the heat to a simmer. Simmer uncovered for at least 1.5 to 2 hours, occasionally skimming off any impurities that float to the surface. After simmering, strain the broth through a fine-mesh strainer, and adjust the seasoning with fish sauce, salt, and sugar to taste.

2. Assemble the Beef Pho:

Cook the rice noodles according to the package instructions and divide them among serving bowls.

Arrange slices of raw beef brisket or sirloin on top of the noodles.

Pour the hot broth over the beef, which will cook it. Ensure the broth is hot enough to fully cook the raw beef slices.

3. Serve:

Serve the Beef Pho hot, accompanied by bean sprouts, fresh herbs, lime wedges, sliced green onions, and chili slices.

Offer hoisin sauce and Sriracha on the side for those who want to add extra flavor and spice.

Enjoy your homemade Beef Pho! It's a comforting and satisfying dish that's perfect for any occasion.

Thai Basil Chicken Noodles

Ingredients:

For the Stir-Fry:

- 8 oz rice noodles, cooked according to package instructions
- 1 lb ground chicken
- 3 tablespoons vegetable oil
- 4 cloves garlic, minced
- 2 Thai bird's eye chilies, finely chopped (adjust to taste)
- 1 bell pepper, thinly sliced
- 1 onion, thinly sliced

For the Sauce:

- 3 tablespoons soy sauce
- 1 tablespoon oyster sauce
- 1 tablespoon fish sauce
- 1 teaspoon sugar
- 1/2 cup fresh Thai basil leaves

For Garnish:

- Lime wedges
- Sliced red chili (optional)
- Chopped green onions

Instructions:

1. Cook the Rice Noodles:

    Cook the rice noodles according to the package instructions. Drain and set aside.

2. Prepare the Sauce:

In a small bowl, mix together soy sauce, oyster sauce, fish sauce, and sugar. Set aside.

3. Stir-Fry:

    Heat vegetable oil in a wok or large skillet over medium-high heat.
    Add minced garlic and chopped Thai bird's eye chilies. Stir-fry for about 30 seconds until fragrant.
    Add ground chicken to the wok and cook until browned and cooked through.
    Add sliced bell pepper and onion to the wok. Stir-fry for an additional 2-3 minutes until the vegetables are tender-crisp.

4. Add Sauce and Thai Basil:

    Pour the prepared sauce over the chicken and vegetables in the wok. Toss everything together until well coated.
    Add fresh Thai basil leaves to the wok and stir-fry until the basil wilts and releases its aroma.

5. Serve:

    Divide the cooked rice noodles among serving plates.
    Spoon the Thai Basil Chicken over the noodles.

6. Garnish and Enjoy:

    Garnish with lime wedges, sliced red chili (if desired), and chopped green onions.
    Serve hot and enjoy your flavorful Thai Basil Chicken Noodles!

Feel free to customize the dish by adding more or less chili according to your spice preference. This dish is quick, easy, and bursting with Thai flavors.

Cold Sesame Noodles

Ingredients:

For the Noodles:

- 8 oz Chinese egg noodles or soba noodles
- 1 tablespoon sesame oil
- 2 tablespoons soy sauce
- 1 tablespoon rice vinegar
- 1 teaspoon sugar
- 1/2 teaspoon chili oil (optional)
- 2 green onions, thinly sliced
- 1 tablespoon sesame seeds, toasted

For the Sesame Sauce:

- 3 tablespoons creamy peanut butter
- 2 tablespoons soy sauce
- 1 tablespoon sesame oil
- 1 tablespoon rice vinegar
- 1 tablespoon honey or maple syrup
- 1 clove garlic, minced
- 1 teaspoon grated ginger
- 2-3 tablespoons water (as needed for desired consistency)

For Garnish:

- Thinly sliced cucumber
- Chopped cilantro
- Crushed peanuts

Instructions:

1. Cook the Noodles:

    Cook the Chinese egg noodles or soba noodles according to the package instructions. Drain and rinse under cold water to stop the cooking process.
    In a bowl, toss the cooked noodles with sesame oil, soy sauce, rice vinegar, sugar, chili oil (if using), sliced green onions, and toasted sesame seeds. Set aside.

2. Prepare the Sesame Sauce:

    In a separate bowl, whisk together peanut butter, soy sauce, sesame oil, rice vinegar, honey or maple syrup, minced garlic, and grated ginger.
    Add water gradually to achieve the desired sauce consistency. The sauce should be smooth and pourable.

3. Combine and Chill:

    Pour the sesame sauce over the seasoned noodles and toss until the noodles are well coated with the sauce.
    Place the noodle mixture in the refrigerator to chill for at least 30 minutes to allow the flavors to meld.

4. Serve:

    Before serving, garnish the Cold Sesame Noodles with thinly sliced cucumber, chopped cilantro, and crushed peanuts.
    Serve chilled and enjoy your delicious Cold Sesame Noodles!

This dish is versatile, and you can add protein such as shredded chicken, tofu, or shrimp if you'd like a heartier meal. Adjust the spice level and other ingredients to suit your taste preferences.

Miso Ramen

Ingredients:

For the Miso Broth:

- 4 cups vegetable or chicken broth
- 3 tablespoons white or red miso paste
- 2 tablespoons soy sauce
- 1 tablespoon mirin (optional)
- 1 tablespoon sesame oil
- 2 cloves garlic, minced
- 1 tablespoon grated ginger

For the Ramen:

- 8 oz ramen noodles
- 1 cup sliced mushrooms (shiitake, button, or your choice)
- 1 cup baby spinach or bok choy, chopped
- 1 cup sliced green onions
- 1 cup tofu cubes or cooked protein of your choice (optional)
- Nori sheets (seaweed), sliced into strips for garnish

Optional Toppings:

- Corn kernels
- Bamboo shoots
- Sesame seeds
- Soft-boiled eggs

Instructions:

1. Prepare the Miso Broth:

   In a pot, heat sesame oil over medium heat. Add minced garlic and grated ginger, sauté for about 1 minute until fragrant.
   Add the vegetable or chicken broth to the pot and bring it to a simmer.

In a small bowl, mix miso paste, soy sauce, and mirin until well combined. Add this miso mixture to the simmering broth and stir until the miso is dissolved. Allow the broth to simmer for about 10-15 minutes to develop the flavors. Adjust the seasoning if needed.

2. Cook the Ramen Noodles:

    Cook the ramen noodles according to the package instructions. Drain and set aside.

3. Assemble the Miso Ramen:

    Divide the cooked ramen noodles among serving bowls.
    Ladle the hot miso broth over the noodles.

4. Add Toppings:

    Add sliced mushrooms, chopped baby spinach or bok choy, green onions, and tofu cubes (or your choice of protein) to each bowl.
    Garnish with nori strips, corn kernels, bamboo shoots, sesame seeds, and soft-boiled eggs if desired.

5. Serve:

    Serve the Miso Ramen hot, and enjoy your homemade Japanese noodle soup!

Feel free to customize this recipe with your favorite toppings and adjust the miso broth to your taste preferences. Miso Ramen is a versatile dish that can be adapted to suit various dietary preferences and cravings.

Chicken Yakitori Udon

Ingredients:

For the Chicken Yakitori:

- 1 lb boneless, skinless chicken thighs, cut into bite-sized pieces
- 1/4 cup soy sauce
- 2 tablespoons mirin
- 1 tablespoon sake (optional)
- 1 tablespoon honey or brown sugar
- 1 clove garlic, minced
- 1 teaspoon grated ginger
- Bamboo skewers, soaked in water for 30 minutes

For the Udon Soup:

- 8 oz udon noodles, cooked according to package instructions
- 4 cups chicken broth
- 2 tablespoons soy sauce
- 1 tablespoon mirin
- 1 tablespoon sake (optional)
- 1 tablespoon sesame oil
- 1 tablespoon sugar
- 2 green onions, sliced
- Nori sheets, sliced into strips for garnish (optional)
- Sesame seeds for garnish (optional)

Instructions:

1. Prepare the Chicken Yakitori:

   In a bowl, mix together soy sauce, mirin, sake, honey or brown sugar, minced garlic, and grated ginger to make the marinade.
   Thread the chicken pieces onto soaked bamboo skewers.
   Brush the chicken skewers with the marinade, making sure they are well-coated. Reserve some marinade for basting during grilling.
   Grill the chicken skewers on a barbecue or grill pan, basting with the reserved marinade, until fully cooked and slightly charred.

2. Cook the Udon Soup:

    In a pot, combine chicken broth, soy sauce, mirin, sake, sesame oil, and sugar. Bring the mixture to a simmer.
    Add the cooked udon noodles to the simmering broth and heat through.
    Adjust the seasoning if needed.

3. Assemble the Chicken Yakitori Udon:

    Divide the udon noodles and broth among serving bowls.
    Remove the chicken skewers from the grill and place them on top of the udon noodles.

4. Garnish and Serve:

    Garnish the Chicken Yakitori Udon with sliced green onions, nori strips, and sesame seeds if desired.
    Serve hot and enjoy your delicious Chicken Yakitori Udon!

Feel free to customize the recipe with additional toppings or vegetables such as spinach, mushrooms, or bean sprouts. Chicken Yakitori Udon is a comforting and satisfying dish with a perfect balance of flavors.

Dan Dan Noodles

Ingredients:

For the Sauce:

- 3 tablespoons soy sauce
- 2 tablespoons Chinese black vinegar
- 1 tablespoon sesame oil
- 1 tablespoon sugar
- 2 teaspoons chili oil (adjust to taste)
- 2 cloves garlic, minced
- 1 teaspoon grated ginger
- 2 tablespoons tahini (sesame paste)
- 2 tablespoons water

For the Noodles:

- 8 oz Chinese egg noodles or wheat noodles
- 1 tablespoon vegetable oil
- 1/2 lb ground pork or chicken
- 2 green onions, finely chopped
- 2 tablespoons Sichuan peppercorns, toasted and ground
- Crushed peanuts for garnish
- Chopped cilantro for garnish

Instructions:

1. Prepare the Sauce:

    In a bowl, whisk together soy sauce, Chinese black vinegar, sesame oil, sugar, chili oil, minced garlic, grated ginger, tahini, and water. Set aside.

2. Cook the Noodles:

    Cook the Chinese egg noodles or wheat noodles according to the package instructions. Drain and set aside.

3. Cook the Meat:

    In a wok or large skillet, heat vegetable oil over medium-high heat.
    Add ground pork or chicken to the wok and cook until browned and cooked through.
    Add finely chopped green onions to the wok and stir-fry for another minute.

4. Assemble the Dan Dan Noodles:

    Divide the cooked noodles among serving bowls.
    Spoon the cooked meat and green onions over the noodles.

5. Add Sauce and Garnish:

    Pour the prepared sauce over the noodles and meat.
    Sprinkle ground Sichuan peppercorns over the top.
    Garnish with crushed peanuts and chopped cilantro.

6. Serve:

    Toss everything together before eating, ensuring that the sauce and toppings are evenly distributed.
    Serve the Dan Dan Noodles hot and enjoy the bold and spicy flavors!

Adjust the spice level and other ingredients according to your taste preferences. Dan Dan Noodles are known for their intense and numbing heat from Sichuan peppercorns, providing a unique and flavorful experience.

Teriyaki Noodle Stir-Fry

Ingredients:

For the Teriyaki Sauce:

- 1/4 cup soy sauce
- 2 tablespoons mirin (or rice wine)
- 2 tablespoons sake (or white wine)
- 2 tablespoons brown sugar
- 1 tablespoon honey
- 1 teaspoon sesame oil
- 1 teaspoon grated ginger
- 1 clove garlic, minced
- 1 tablespoon cornstarch mixed with 2 tablespoons water (optional, for thickening)

For the Stir-Fry:

- 8 oz soba noodles or udon noodles, cooked according to package instructions
- 2 tablespoons vegetable oil
- 1 lb mixed vegetables (broccoli, bell peppers, carrots, snap peas, etc.), chopped
- 1 cup firm tofu or cooked chicken, sliced
- Sesame seeds and chopped green onions for garnish

Instructions:

1. Prepare the Teriyaki Sauce:

    In a bowl, whisk together soy sauce, mirin, sake, brown sugar, honey, sesame oil, grated ginger, and minced garlic.
    If you prefer a thicker sauce, mix 1 tablespoon of cornstarch with 2 tablespoons of water to create a slurry. Add this to the sauce mixture.

2. Cook the Noodles:

    Cook the soba or udon noodles according to the package instructions. Drain and set aside.

3. Stir-Fry:

Heat vegetable oil in a large skillet or wok over medium-high heat.
Add the mixed vegetables to the skillet and stir-fry for 3-5 minutes until they are tender-crisp.
Add tofu or cooked chicken to the skillet and cook for an additional 2-3 minutes until heated through.
Add the cooked noodles to the skillet and pour the teriyaki sauce over the noodles and vegetables.
Toss everything together until the noodles and vegetables are evenly coated with the teriyaki sauce.

4. Garnish and Serve:

Garnish the Teriyaki Noodle Stir-Fry with sesame seeds and chopped green onions.
Serve hot and enjoy your delicious and quick teriyaki noodle stir-fry!

Feel free to customize this recipe by adding your favorite vegetables or protein options. Adjust the sweetness or saltiness of the teriyaki sauce to suit your taste preferences.

Szechuan Spicy Noodles

Ingredients:

For the Sauce:

- 3 tablespoons soy sauce
- 2 tablespoons Chinese black vinegar
- 2 tablespoons sesame oil
- 2 tablespoons tahini (sesame paste)
- 1 tablespoon sugar
- 2 teaspoons Sichuan peppercorn powder
- 2 teaspoons chili oil (adjust to taste)
- 2 cloves garlic, minced
- 1 teaspoon grated ginger
- 2 green onions, finely chopped

For the Noodles:

- 8 oz Chinese wheat noodles or egg noodles
- 2 tablespoons vegetable oil
- 1/4 cup ground pork or meat of your choice (optional)
- 1 cup baby bok choy or Chinese greens, chopped
- 1/4 cup roasted peanuts, crushed
- Chopped cilantro for garnish

Instructions:

1. Prepare the Sauce:

    In a bowl, mix together soy sauce, Chinese black vinegar, sesame oil, tahini, sugar, Sichuan peppercorn powder, chili oil, minced garlic, grated ginger, and chopped green onions. Set aside.

2. Cook the Noodles:

Cook the Chinese wheat noodles or egg noodles according to the package instructions. Drain and set aside.

3. Stir-Fry:

   Heat vegetable oil in a wok or large skillet over medium-high heat.
   If using ground pork or meat, add it to the wok and stir-fry until cooked through.
   Add the chopped baby bok choy or Chinese greens to the wok and stir-fry for 2-3 minutes until they are slightly wilted.

4. Assemble the Szechuan Spicy Noodles:

   Divide the cooked noodles among serving bowls.
   Spoon the stir-fried meat and vegetables over the noodles.

5. Add Sauce and Garnish:

   Pour the prepared sauce over the noodles, meat, and vegetables.
   Garnish with crushed roasted peanuts and chopped cilantro.

6. Serve:

   Toss everything together before eating to ensure the sauce is evenly distributed.
   Serve the Szechuan Spicy Noodles hot and enjoy the bold and spicy flavors!

Adjust the spice level and other ingredients according to your taste preferences.

Szechuan Spicy Noodles are known for their numbing heat and rich flavors, making them a favorite among lovers of spicy cuisine.

Indonesian Bakmi Goreng

Ingredients:

For the Noodles:

- 8 oz egg noodles, cooked according to package instructions
- 2 tablespoons vegetable oil
- 2 cloves garlic, minced
- 1 small onion, finely chopped
- 1 chicken breast, thinly sliced
- 1 cup shrimp, peeled and deveined
- 2 eggs, lightly beaten
- 1 cup cabbage, shredded
- 1 carrot, julienned
- 2 green onions, sliced
- 1 tablespoon sweet soy sauce (kecap manis)
- 2 tablespoons soy sauce
- 1 tablespoon oyster sauce
- Salt and pepper to taste

For Garnish:

- Fried shallots (optional)
- Sliced red chilies (optional)
- Lime wedges

Instructions:

1. Prepare the Noodles:

    Cook the egg noodles according to the package instructions. Drain and set aside.

2. Stir-Fry:

    Heat vegetable oil in a wok or large skillet over medium-high heat.
    Add minced garlic and chopped onion. Sauté until fragrant and the onion becomes translucent.
    Add sliced chicken to the wok and cook until it's no longer pink.
    Add shrimp to the wok and cook until they turn pink and opaque.

Push the chicken and shrimp to one side of the wok, add the beaten eggs to the empty space, and scramble them until cooked.
Mix everything together in the wok and add shredded cabbage, julienned carrot, and sliced green onions. Stir-fry for a few minutes until the vegetables are tender-crisp.

3. Season and Finish:

    Add cooked egg noodles to the wok.
    Pour sweet soy sauce, soy sauce, and oyster sauce over the noodles and toss everything together until well combined.
    Season with salt and pepper to taste.

4. Garnish and Serve:

    Garnish the Bakmi Goreng with fried shallots and sliced red chilies if desired.
    Serve hot with lime wedges on the side.

Enjoy your flavorful Indonesian Bakmi Goreng! This dish is often enjoyed with additional condiments like sambal (chili paste) for those who like an extra kick of spice.

Thai Drunken Noodles

Ingredients:

For the Sauce:

- 3 tablespoons soy sauce
- 1 tablespoon oyster sauce
- 1 tablespoon fish sauce
- 1 tablespoon sweet soy sauce (or brown sugar as a substitute)
- 1 teaspoon chili paste (adjust to taste)
- 2 cloves garlic, minced

For the Noodles:

- 8 oz wide rice noodles, soaked in warm water until softened
- 2 tablespoons vegetable oil
- 1 lb chicken, beef, shrimp, or tofu, thinly sliced
- 1 bell pepper, sliced
- 1 onion, thinly sliced
- 1 cup Thai basil leaves
- 2 tomatoes, cut into wedges
- 2 eggs (optional)
- Lime wedges for serving

Instructions:

1. Prepare the Sauce:

    In a bowl, whisk together soy sauce, oyster sauce, fish sauce, sweet soy sauce (or brown sugar), chili paste, and minced garlic. Set aside.

2. Stir-Fry:

    Heat vegetable oil in a wok or large skillet over medium-high heat.
    Add the sliced protein (chicken, beef, shrimp, or tofu) to the wok and stir-fry until cooked through.
    Push the cooked protein to one side of the wok, crack the eggs into the empty space (if using), and scramble until just cooked.

Add sliced bell pepper and onion to the wok. Stir-fry for 2-3 minutes until the vegetables are tender-crisp.

3. Add Noodles and Sauce:

    Add the soaked and softened rice noodles to the wok.
    Pour the prepared sauce over the noodles and toss everything together until well combined.

4. Thai Basil and Tomatoes:

    Add Thai basil leaves and tomato wedges to the wok. Toss for an additional 1-2 minutes until the basil wilts and the tomatoes soften slightly.

5. Serve:

    Serve the Thai Drunken Noodles hot, garnished with additional Thai basil leaves and lime wedges on the side.
    Enjoy your flavorful and spicy Thai Drunken Noodles!

Feel free to customize the protein and vegetables according to your preferences. The dish is traditionally spicy, but you can adjust the heat level to suit your taste.

Tempura Soba

Ingredients:

For the Tempura:

- Assorted vegetables (such as sweet potatoes, zucchini, mushrooms, and bell peppers), thinly sliced
- Seafood (shrimp, squid, or white fish), cleaned and deveined
- 1 cup all-purpose flour, for coating
- Ice-cold water (enough to make a thin batter)
- Vegetable oil for frying

For the Soba Noodles:

- 8 oz soba noodles
- 6 cups water for boiling
- Ice water for rinsing

For the Dipping Sauce (Tsuyu):

- 2 cups dashi stock (or use a mixture of water and instant dashi powder)
- 1/3 cup soy sauce
- 1/3 cup mirin
- 1 tablespoon sugar

For Garnish:

- Grated daikon radish
- Chopped green onions
- Wasabi

Instructions:

1. Prepare the Dipping Sauce (Tsuyu):

In a saucepan, combine dashi stock, soy sauce, mirin, and sugar. Bring to a simmer over medium heat, stirring until the sugar dissolves. Allow it to cool, then refrigerate until ready to use.

2. Cook the Soba Noodles:

Bring 6 cups of water to a boil in a large pot.
Add soba noodles to the boiling water and cook according to the package instructions (usually around 4-5 minutes).
Drain the noodles and rinse them under cold running water or in a bowl of ice water to stop the cooking process. Set aside.

3. Prepare the Tempura:

Heat vegetable oil in a deep fryer or a large, deep pan to 350-375°F (180-190°C).
In a bowl, mix all-purpose flour with ice-cold water to create a thin batter.
Dip the sliced vegetables and seafood into the tempura batter, making sure they are well coated.
Carefully place the coated items into the hot oil and fry until golden and crispy. Work in batches to avoid overcrowding.
Remove the tempura from the oil and drain on paper towels.

4. Assemble Tempura Soba:

Divide the cooked and rinsed soba noodles among serving bowls.
Arrange the tempura over the soba noodles.

5. Serve:

Serve the Tempura Soba with the chilled dipping sauce (Tsuyu).
Garnish with grated daikon radish, chopped green onions, and a dollop of wasabi.
Enjoy your homemade Tempura Soba by dipping the tempura into the flavorful sauce and savoring the combination of crispy tempura and refreshing soba noodles.

Beef and Broccoli Noodles

Ingredients:

For the Beef Marinade:

- 1 lb flank steak, thinly sliced against the grain
- 2 tablespoons soy sauce
- 1 tablespoon oyster sauce
- 1 tablespoon cornstarch
- 1 tablespoon vegetable oil

For the Noodles:

- 8 oz lo mein noodles or your favorite noodles, cooked according to package instructions
- 2 tablespoons vegetable oil

For the Stir-Fry:

- 3 cups broccoli florets
- 3 cloves garlic, minced
- 1 tablespoon ginger, grated
- 1/4 cup soy sauce
- 2 tablespoons oyster sauce
- 1 tablespoon hoisin sauce
- 1 tablespoon brown sugar
- 1 tablespoon cornstarch mixed with 2 tablespoons water (optional, for thickening)
- Sesame seeds and sliced green onions for garnish

Instructions:

1. Marinate the Beef:

In a bowl, combine thinly sliced flank steak with soy sauce, oyster sauce, cornstarch, and vegetable oil. Mix well and let it marinate for at least 15-20 minutes.

2. Cook the Noodles:

Cook the lo mein noodles or your chosen noodles according to the package instructions. Drain and set aside.

3. Stir-Fry:

Heat 2 tablespoons of vegetable oil in a wok or large skillet over medium-high heat.
Add marinated beef to the wok and stir-fry until it's browned and cooked through. Remove the beef from the wok and set it aside.
In the same wok, add more oil if needed. Stir in minced garlic and grated ginger, and sauté for about 30 seconds until fragrant.
Add broccoli florets to the wok and stir-fry for 2-3 minutes until they are crisp-tender.

4. Combine and Sauce:

Return the cooked beef to the wok with the broccoli.
In a small bowl, mix soy sauce, oyster sauce, hoisin sauce, brown sugar, and the optional cornstarch-water mixture. Pour this sauce over the beef and broccoli.
Toss everything together until the beef and broccoli are coated with the sauce.

5. Add Noodles and Garnish:

Add the cooked noodles to the wok and toss until they are well combined with the beef, broccoli, and sauce.
Garnish with sesame seeds and sliced green onions.

6. Serve:

Serve the Beef and Broccoli Noodles hot, and enjoy your delicious and flavorful meal!

Feel free to customize this recipe by adding other vegetables or adjusting the sauce according to your taste preferences. It's a versatile dish that's quick and easy to make at home.

Hainanese Chicken Rice Noodles

Ingredients:

For the Chicken:

- 1 whole chicken (about 3-4 pounds)
- 4 slices ginger
- 3 stalks green onions, cut into 2-inch pieces
- Salt, to taste

For the Rice Noodles:

- Rice noodles (flat or vermicelli), cooked according to package instructions

For the Chicken Rice:

- 2 cups jasmine rice
- 4 cups chicken broth (from poaching the chicken)
- 2 cloves garlic, minced
- 2 tablespoons vegetable oil
- Salt, to taste

For the Dipping Sauce:

- 2 tablespoons soy sauce
- 1 tablespoon oyster sauce
- 1 tablespoon sesame oil
- 1 tablespoon chicken broth (from poaching the chicken)
- Fresh cilantro, chopped (for garnish)

For Garnish:

- Fresh cucumber slices
- Fresh cilantro
- Sliced green onions
- Chili sauce or freshly chopped red chilies (optional)

Instructions:

1. Poach the Chicken:

    In a large pot, bring water to a boil. Add slices of ginger, green onion pieces, and salt.
    Carefully place the whole chicken into the pot, breast side down. Reduce the heat to a simmer and poach the chicken for about 40-50 minutes or until cooked through.
    Once cooked, remove the chicken from the pot and let it rest. Save the chicken broth for cooking rice and making the dipping sauce.

2. Cook the Rice:

    Rinse jasmine rice under cold water until the water runs clear.
    In a saucepan, heat vegetable oil over medium heat. Add minced garlic and sauté until fragrant.
    Add the rinsed rice to the saucepan and stir for a few minutes until the rice is well-coated with the garlic-infused oil.
    Pour in the chicken broth (from poaching the chicken) and bring to a boil. Reduce heat to low, cover, and simmer until the rice is cooked.

3. Prepare the Dipping Sauce:

    In a small bowl, mix soy sauce, oyster sauce, sesame oil, and a tablespoon of chicken broth from poaching the chicken. Set aside.

4. Assemble the Dish:

    Slice the poached chicken into bite-sized pieces.
    Arrange the cooked rice noodles on serving plates, top with slices of poached chicken, and garnish with cucumber slices, cilantro, and sliced green onions.
    Drizzle the dipping sauce over the chicken and noodles.

5. Serve:

    Serve the Hainanese Chicken Rice Noodles hot, accompanied by chili sauce if desired.
    Enjoy this flavorful and comforting dish!

Feel free to adjust the seasoning and ingredients to suit your taste preferences. Hainanese Chicken Rice Noodles is a versatile and comforting dish that's perfect for any occasion.

Bibimbap Noodles

Ingredients:

For the Noodles:

- 8 oz Korean sweet potato noodles (dangmyeon) or any Asian noodles of your choice
- 2 tablespoons soy sauce
- 1 tablespoon sesame oil
- 1 tablespoon sugar
- 1 teaspoon minced garlic
- 1 tablespoon vegetable oil for cooking

For the Bibimbap Toppings:

- 1 cup cooked and shredded beef or chicken (marinated with soy sauce, sesame oil, and a bit of sugar)
- 2 cups julienned or sliced vegetables (carrots, spinach, zucchini, mushrooms, bean sprouts)
- 4 fried eggs (cooked sunny-side-up)
- Kimchi
- Sesame seeds for garnish
- Sliced green onions for garnish

For the Gochujang Sauce:

- 3 tablespoons gochujang (Korean red pepper paste)
- 1 tablespoon soy sauce
- 1 tablespoon sesame oil
- 1 tablespoon sugar
- 1 tablespoon water

Instructions:

1. Cook the Noodles:

Boil the sweet potato noodles (dangmyeon) or your chosen noodles according to the package instructions. Drain and rinse under cold water to cool them down.
In a bowl, mix the cooked noodles with soy sauce, sesame oil, sugar, and minced garlic. Set aside.

2. Prepare the Gochujang Sauce:

   In a small bowl, whisk together gochujang, soy sauce, sesame oil, sugar, and water until well combined. Set aside.

3. Cook the Toppings:

   Heat vegetable oil in a pan over medium heat.
   Cook the shredded beef or chicken until fully cooked and well-marinated. Set aside.
   In the same pan, stir-fry the julienned or sliced vegetables until they are cooked but still crisp. Set aside.

4. Assemble the Bibimbap Noodles:

   Divide the seasoned noodles among serving bowls.
   Arrange the cooked and shredded beef or chicken, stir-fried vegetables, fried eggs, and kimchi on top of the noodles.

5. Serve with Gochujang Sauce:

   Drizzle the prepared gochujang sauce over the Bibimbap Noodles.
   Garnish with sesame seeds and sliced green onions.

6. Serve:

   Serve the Bibimbap Noodles immediately, mixing everything together before eating to enjoy the combination of flavors and textures.
   Enjoy your delicious Bibimbap Noodles!

Feel free to customize the toppings based on your preferences. Bibimbap Noodles offer a tasty and satisfying meal with a perfect balance of sweet, savory, and spicy flavors.

Burmese Coconut Noodle Soup

Ingredients:

For the Coconut Broth:

- 1 can (14 oz) coconut milk
- 4 cups chicken or vegetable broth
- 1 onion, finely chopped
- 3 cloves garlic, minced
- 1 tablespoon ginger, grated
- 1 tablespoon curry powder
- 1 teaspoon turmeric powder
- 1 tablespoon fish sauce
- 1 tablespoon soy sauce
- Salt and pepper to taste

For the Soup:

- 8 oz egg noodles or rice noodles, cooked according to package instructions
- 1 lb chicken breast, thinly sliced
- 1 cup coconut cream (the thick part at the top of a separated can of coconut milk)
- 2 tablespoons vegetable oil
- 1 onion, thinly sliced
- 2 hard-boiled eggs, sliced
- Fresh cilantro, chopped (for garnish)
- Lime wedges

For Toppings (Optional):

- Crispy fried noodles
- Fried garlic
- Sliced green onions
- Chili flakes

Instructions:

1. Prepare the Coconut Broth:

   In a large pot, heat vegetable oil over medium heat.
   Add chopped onion, minced garlic, and grated ginger. Sauté until the onions are translucent.
   Stir in curry powder and turmeric powder, and cook for another minute until fragrant.
   Pour in coconut milk, chicken or vegetable broth, fish sauce, soy sauce, salt, and pepper. Bring to a simmer and let it cook for about 15-20 minutes.

2. Cook the Chicken:

   In a separate pan, heat 2 tablespoons of vegetable oil over medium heat.
   Add thinly sliced chicken breast and cook until browned and cooked through.

3. Assemble the Soup:

   Add the cooked chicken to the coconut broth.
   Stir in coconut cream and let it simmer for an additional 5 minutes.

4. Serve:

   Divide the cooked noodles among serving bowls.
   Ladle the coconut broth with chicken over the noodles.
   Top each bowl with sliced onions, hard-boiled egg slices, chopped cilantro, and any optional toppings you desire.
   Serve the Burmese Coconut Noodle Soup hot, with lime wedges on the side.

Enjoy the rich and aromatic flavors of this Burmese Coconut Noodle Soup! Adjust the seasonings and spice levels according to your preferences.

Kimchi Udon

Ingredients:

For the Kimchi Udon:

- 8 oz udon noodles, cooked according to package instructions
- 1 cup kimchi, chopped
- 1 cup firm tofu, cubed
- 2 tablespoons vegetable oil
- 2 cloves garlic, minced
- 1 tablespoon ginger, grated
- 2 green onions, sliced
- 2 tablespoons soy sauce
- 1 tablespoon sesame oil
- 1 tablespoon gochugaru (Korean red pepper flakes, adjust to taste)
- 1 tablespoon rice vinegar
- 1 teaspoon sugar
- Sesame seeds for garnish

Instructions:

1. Prepare the Udon Noodles:

    Cook the udon noodles according to the package instructions. Drain and set aside.

2. Cook the Tofu:

    Heat 1 tablespoon of vegetable oil in a pan over medium heat.
    Add cubed tofu and cook until golden brown on all sides. Remove from the pan and set aside.

3. Cook the Kimchi Udon:

    In the same pan, add another tablespoon of vegetable oil.
    Add minced garlic and grated ginger. Sauté until fragrant.

Add chopped kimchi and stir-fry for 2-3 minutes.
Mix in soy sauce, sesame oil, gochugaru, rice vinegar, and sugar. Stir well to combine.
Add the cooked udon noodles and tofu to the pan. Toss everything together until well coated with the kimchi mixture.

4. Garnish and Serve:

Garnish the Kimchi Udon with sliced green onions and sesame seeds.
Serve hot and enjoy your delicious Kimchi Udon!

Feel free to customize the recipe by adding other vegetables or protein sources. Adjust the level of spiciness to your liking. This fusion dish brings together the tangy and spicy flavors of kimchi with the comforting chewiness of udon noodles.

Satay Chicken Noodles

Ingredients:

For the Satay Sauce:

- 1/2 cup creamy peanut butter
- 2 tablespoons soy sauce
- 1 tablespoon honey
- 1 tablespoon rice vinegar
- 1 teaspoon sesame oil
- 1 teaspoon minced garlic
- 1 teaspoon grated ginger
- 1/2 teaspoon chili flakes (adjust to taste)
- 1/2 cup coconut milk
- Salt and pepper to taste

For the Chicken:

- 1 lb boneless, skinless chicken breasts or thighs, thinly sliced
- Salt and pepper to taste
- 1 tablespoon vegetable oil

For the Noodles:

- 8 oz egg noodles or rice noodles, cooked according to package instructions

For the Stir-Fry:

- 2 tablespoons vegetable oil
- 1 red bell pepper, thinly sliced
- 1 carrot, julienned
- 1 cup snow peas, trimmed
- 2 green onions, sliced
- Fresh cilantro for garnish
- Crushed peanuts for garnish

Instructions:

1. Prepare the Satay Sauce:

    In a bowl, whisk together peanut butter, soy sauce, honey, rice vinegar, sesame oil, minced garlic, grated ginger, chili flakes, and coconut milk until smooth. Season with salt and pepper to taste. Adjust the consistency by adding more coconut milk if needed. Set aside.

2. Cook the Chicken:

    Season the thinly sliced chicken with salt and pepper.
    In a large skillet or wok, heat 1 tablespoon of vegetable oil over medium-high heat.
    Add the seasoned chicken and cook until browned and cooked through. Remove the chicken from the skillet and set aside.

3. Prepare the Noodles:

    Cook the egg noodles or rice noodles according to the package instructions. Drain and set aside.

4. Stir-Fry:

    In the same skillet or wok, add 2 tablespoons of vegetable oil over medium-high heat.
    Add sliced red bell pepper, julienned carrot, and snow peas. Stir-fry for 2-3 minutes until the vegetables are crisp-tender.
    Add the cooked chicken back to the skillet.
    Pour the prepared satay sauce over the chicken and vegetables. Toss everything together until well coated.

5. Assemble:

    Divide the cooked noodles among serving plates.
    Top the noodles with the satay chicken and vegetable mixture.

6. Garnish:

   Garnish the Satay Chicken Noodles with sliced green onions, fresh cilantro, and crushed peanuts.
   Serve hot and enjoy your delicious Satay Chicken Noodles!

Feel free to customize the recipe by adding other vegetables or adjusting the spice level.

This dish offers a perfect combination of creamy, nutty satay sauce with the satisfying texture of noodles and tender chicken.

Hot and Sour Glass Noodle Soup

Ingredients:

For the Broth:

- 6 cups vegetable or chicken broth
- 3 tablespoons soy sauce
- 2 tablespoons rice vinegar
- 1 tablespoon chili garlic sauce (adjust to taste for spice level)
- 1 tablespoon ginger, grated
- 2 cloves garlic, minced
- 1 tablespoon sugar
- Salt and pepper to taste

For the Soup:

- 4 oz dried glass noodles (also known as mung bean noodles or cellophane noodles)
- 1 cup tofu, cubed
- 1 cup shiitake mushrooms, sliced
- 1 cup bamboo shoots, julienned
- 1 cup baby corn, cut into bite-sized pieces
- 1 cup bok choy, chopped
- 1 cup firm tofu, cubed (optional)
- 2 green onions, sliced
- Fresh cilantro for garnish
- Lime wedges for serving

Instructions:

1. Prepare the Broth:

    In a large pot, combine vegetable or chicken broth, soy sauce, rice vinegar, chili garlic sauce, grated ginger, minced garlic, sugar, salt, and pepper.
    Bring the broth to a simmer over medium heat. Taste and adjust the seasoning if necessary.

2. Prepare the Glass Noodles:

In a separate bowl, soak the dried glass noodles in hot water according to the package instructions until they are softened. Drain and set aside.

3. Assemble the Soup:

    Add tofu, shiitake mushrooms, bamboo shoots, baby corn, and bok choy to the simmering broth. Cook for 5-7 minutes or until the vegetables are tender.
    If using firm tofu, add it to the soup during the last 2-3 minutes of cooking.
    Add the soaked glass noodles to the pot and cook for an additional 2-3 minutes until the noodles are heated through.

4. Serve:

    Ladle the Hot and Sour Glass Noodle Soup into bowls.
    Garnish with sliced green onions, fresh cilantro, and lime wedges.
    Serve hot and enjoy the comforting and flavorful soup!

Feel free to customize this recipe by adding other vegetables or adjusting the spice level according to your preferences. Hot and Sour Glass Noodle Soup is a hearty and satisfying dish perfect for any time of the year.

Japanese Curry Udon

Ingredients:

For the Curry Broth:

- 1 tablespoon vegetable oil
- 1 onion, thinly sliced
- 2 carrots, julienned
- 2 potatoes, peeled and diced
- 1-2 tablespoons curry powder (Japanese curry powder if available)
- 4 cups vegetable or chicken broth
- 2 tablespoons soy sauce
- 2 tablespoons mirin
- 2 tablespoons sake (optional)
- 2 teaspoons sugar
- Salt and pepper to taste

For the Udon Noodles:

- 8 oz fresh or frozen udon noodles (cooked according to package instructions)

Optional Toppings:

- Sliced green onions
- Tempura crumbs (tenkasu)
- Red pickled ginger (beni shoga)
- Shichimi togarashi (Japanese seven-spice blend)

Instructions:

1. Prepare the Curry Broth:

    In a large pot, heat vegetable oil over medium heat. Add sliced onions and cook until softened.
    Add julienned carrots and diced potatoes to the pot. Sauté for a few minutes until the vegetables are slightly tender.

Sprinkle curry powder over the vegetables and stir to coat evenly.
Pour in vegetable or chicken broth, soy sauce, mirin, sake (if using), sugar, salt, and pepper. Bring the mixture to a simmer and let it cook until the vegetables are fully cooked and the broth is flavorful.

2. Cook the Udon Noodles:

While the curry broth is simmering, cook the udon noodles according to the package instructions. If using fresh udon, it usually takes a few minutes, while frozen udon may take a bit longer.
Drain the udon noodles and set them aside.

3. Assemble the Japanese Curry Udon:

Place a portion of cooked udon noodles into serving bowls.
Ladle the hot curry broth with vegetables over the udon noodles.

4. Garnish:

Garnish the Japanese Curry Udon with sliced green onions, tempura crumbs (tenkasu), red pickled ginger (beni shoga), and a sprinkle of shichimi togarashi if you like it spicy.
Serve hot and enjoy your comforting Japanese Curry Udon!

Feel free to adjust the curry powder and seasonings according to your taste preferences. This dish is not only delicious but also customizable with your favorite toppings.

Vietnamese Bun Thit Nuong

Ingredients:

For the Grilled Pork:

- 1 lb pork shoulder or pork loin, thinly sliced
- 3 tablespoons soy sauce
- 2 tablespoons fish sauce
- 2 tablespoons honey or sugar
- 1 tablespoon vegetable oil
- 2 cloves garlic, minced
- 1 shallot, minced
- 1 teaspoon lemongrass, finely chopped (optional)

For the Nuoc Cham Sauce:

- 3 tablespoons fish sauce
- 3 tablespoons rice vinegar
- 3 tablespoons sugar
- 1/2 cup water
- 2 cloves garlic, minced
- 1 red chili, finely chopped (optional)

For the Noodles and Garnishes:

- 8 oz rice vermicelli noodles, cooked according to package instructions
- Lettuce, shredded
- Cucumber, julienned
- Bean sprouts
- Fresh mint leaves
- Fresh cilantro leaves
- Crushed peanuts
- Lime wedges

Instructions:

1. Marinate and Grill the Pork:

    In a bowl, combine soy sauce, fish sauce, honey (or sugar), vegetable oil, minced garlic, minced shallot, and lemongrass (if using).
    Add the thinly sliced pork to the marinade, ensuring each piece is coated. Let it marinate for at least 30 minutes to an hour.
    Grill the marinated pork slices until cooked through and slightly charred. You can use a grill pan, outdoor grill, or broil in the oven.

2. Prepare the Nuoc Cham Sauce:

    In a bowl, whisk together fish sauce, rice vinegar, sugar, water, minced garlic, and chopped chili (if using). Adjust the sweetness, sourness, and spiciness to your liking.
    Set aside the nuoc cham sauce for serving.

3. Assemble the Bun Thit Nuong:

    Arrange a handful of cooked rice vermicelli noodles in each serving bowl.
    Top the noodles with shredded lettuce, julienned cucumber, bean sprouts, and fresh herbs (mint and cilantro).
    Place grilled pork slices on top of the noodles and vegetables.

4. Garnish and Serve:

    Sprinkle crushed peanuts over the top.
    Serve Bun Thit Nuong with lime wedges on the side and the prepared nuoc cham sauce for drizzling.
    Toss everything together before eating to mix the flavors and textures.
    Enjoy your delicious Bun Thit Nuong!

Feel free to customize the toppings and adjust the nuoc cham sauce according to your taste preferences. Bun Thit Nuong is a refreshing and flavorful Vietnamese dish that's perfect for warm weather.

Ginger Scallion Noodles

Ingredients:

For the Noodles:

- 8 oz noodles of your choice (such as spaghetti or egg noodles), cooked according to package instructions

For the Ginger Scallion Sauce:

- 1/2 cup scallions (green onions), finely chopped
- 2 tablespoons fresh ginger, minced
- 2 cloves garlic, minced
- 3 tablespoons soy sauce
- 2 tablespoons sesame oil
- 1 tablespoon rice vinegar
- 1 tablespoon sugar
- 1 teaspoon red pepper flakes (optional, for heat)

For Garnish:

- Additional chopped scallions
- Sesame seeds

Instructions:

1. Cook the Noodles:

    Cook the noodles according to the package instructions. Drain and set aside.

2. Prepare the Ginger Scallion Sauce:

    In a bowl, combine finely chopped scallions, minced ginger, minced garlic, soy sauce, sesame oil, rice vinegar, sugar, and red pepper flakes (if using).
    Mix the ingredients well to create the ginger scallion sauce.

3. Assemble the Ginger Scallion Noodles:

    Toss the cooked noodles with the prepared ginger scallion sauce until the noodles are well coated.
    Mix in additional chopped scallions and sesame seeds for added flavor and texture.

4. Garnish and Serve:

    Garnish the Ginger Scallion Noodles with extra chopped scallions and sesame seeds.
    Serve the noodles at room temperature or slightly chilled.
    Enjoy your simple and flavorful Ginger Scallion Noodles!

Feel free to customize the dish by adding proteins like grilled chicken, shrimp, or tofu if desired. This dish is quick to make and bursting with the vibrant flavors of ginger and scallions.

Teriyaki Chicken Ramen

Ingredients:

For the Teriyaki Chicken:

- 1 lb boneless, skinless chicken thighs, cut into bite-sized pieces
- 1/4 cup soy sauce
- 2 tablespoons mirin
- 1 tablespoon sake (optional)
- 1 tablespoon honey
- 1 teaspoon sesame oil
- 2 cloves garlic, minced
- 1 teaspoon ginger, grated
- 1 tablespoon vegetable oil for cooking

For the Ramen:

- 8 oz ramen noodles, cooked according to package instructions
- 4 cups chicken broth
- 2 tablespoons soy sauce
- 1 tablespoon mirin
- 1 tablespoon sake (optional)
- 1 tablespoon sugar
- 1 tablespoon sesame oil

For Toppings:

- Sliced green onions
- Sesame seeds
- Nori (seaweed) strips
- Soft-boiled eggs, halved

Instructions:

1. Prepare the Teriyaki Chicken:

In a bowl, mix soy sauce, mirin, sake (if using), honey, sesame oil, minced garlic, and grated ginger to create the teriyaki marinade.
Add the chicken pieces to the marinade and let them marinate for at least 30 minutes.
Heat vegetable oil in a pan over medium-high heat. Cook the marinated chicken until browned and cooked through. Set aside.

2. Cook the Ramen:

In a pot, bring chicken broth to a simmer over medium heat.
Add soy sauce, mirin, sake (if using), sugar, and sesame oil to the broth. Adjust the seasoning to taste.
Add cooked ramen noodles to the broth and heat through.

3. Assemble the Teriyaki Chicken Ramen:

Divide the ramen and broth into serving bowls.
Top each bowl with the cooked teriyaki chicken.

4. Garnish:

Garnish the Teriyaki Chicken Ramen with sliced green onions, sesame seeds, nori strips, and soft-boiled eggs.
Serve hot and enjoy your delicious Teriyaki Chicken Ramen!

Feel free to customize this recipe by adding vegetables like spinach, mushrooms, or bok choy to the ramen. Teriyaki Chicken Ramen is a flavorful and satisfying dish that's perfect for a cozy meal at home.

Pineapple Fried Rice Noodles

Ingredients:

For the Rice Noodles:

- 8 oz rice noodles, soaked and cooked according to package instructions
- 2 tablespoons vegetable oil

For the Stir-Fry:

- 1 cup pineapple chunks, fresh or canned
- 1 cup firm tofu, cubed
- 1 red bell pepper, thinly sliced
- 1 carrot, julienned
- 1 cup snap peas, trimmed
- 3 green onions, sliced
- 2 cloves garlic, minced
- 1 tablespoon ginger, grated
- 2 tablespoons soy sauce
- 1 tablespoon oyster sauce
- 1 tablespoon fish sauce (optional for non-vegetarian version)
- 1 tablespoon sesame oil
- 1 tablespoon brown sugar
- 1/2 teaspoon chili flakes (adjust to taste)
- Salt and pepper to taste

For Garnish:

- Fresh cilantro, chopped
- Lime wedges

Instructions:

1. Prepare the Rice Noodles:

    Soak the rice noodles in warm water according to the package instructions until they are pliable.
    Cook the soaked rice noodles in boiling water for a few minutes until they are al dente. Drain and set aside.

2. Stir-Fry:

   Heat vegetable oil in a wok or large pan over medium-high heat.
   Add cubed tofu and stir-fry until golden brown. Remove tofu from the pan and set aside.
   In the same pan, add a bit more oil if needed. Stir-fry garlic and ginger until fragrant.
   Add sliced bell pepper, julienned carrot, and snap peas. Cook for 2-3 minutes until the vegetables are slightly tender but still crisp.
   Add cooked rice noodles to the pan and toss with the vegetables.

3. Pineapple and Sauce:

   Add pineapple chunks and cooked tofu to the pan.
   In a small bowl, mix soy sauce, oyster sauce, fish sauce (if using), sesame oil, brown sugar, and chili flakes. Pour the sauce over the noodles and stir-fry until everything is well coated.
   Season with salt and pepper to taste.

4. Garnish and Serve:

   Garnish the Pineapple Fried Rice Noodles with sliced green onions and chopped cilantro.
   Serve hot with lime wedges on the side.
   Enjoy your delicious Pineapple Fried Rice Noodles!

Feel free to customize this recipe by adding protein such as shrimp or chicken, and adjust the spice level according to your taste preferences. Pineapple Fried Rice Noodles make for a tasty and vibrant meal with a perfect balance of sweet and savory flavors.

Thai Red Curry Noodles

Ingredients:

For the Red Curry Sauce:

- 2 tablespoons red curry paste
- 1 can (14 oz) coconut milk
- 2 tablespoons soy sauce
- 1 tablespoon brown sugar
- 1 tablespoon vegetable oil
- 1 tablespoon ginger, grated
- 2 cloves garlic, minced
- 1 tablespoon lime juice
- 1 tablespoon fish sauce (optional, for non-vegetarian version)
- Salt and pepper to taste

For the Noodles and Vegetables:

- 8 oz rice noodles, cooked according to package instructions
- 1 tablespoon vegetable oil
- 1 red bell pepper, thinly sliced
- 1 carrot, julienned
- 1 zucchini, julienned
- 1 cup broccoli florets
- 1 cup snap peas, trimmed
- 1 cup tofu, cubed (optional, for protein)

For Garnish:

- Fresh cilantro, chopped
- Thai basil leaves
- Lime wedges

Instructions:

1. Prepare the Red Curry Sauce:

In a bowl, mix red curry paste, coconut milk, soy sauce, brown sugar, vegetable oil, grated ginger, minced garlic, lime juice, and fish sauce (if using). Whisk until well combined.

Season with salt and pepper to taste. Set aside.

2. Cook the Noodles and Vegetables:

Cook rice noodles according to the package instructions. Drain and set aside.
In a large pan or wok, heat vegetable oil over medium-high heat.
Add sliced bell pepper, julienned carrot, julienned zucchini, broccoli florets, and snap peas to the pan. Stir-fry for 3-4 minutes until the vegetables are tender-crisp.
If using tofu, add cubed tofu to the pan and cook until lightly browned.

3. Combine and Simmer:

Pour the prepared red curry sauce over the vegetables and tofu.
Add cooked rice noodles to the pan and toss everything together until the noodles are well coated with the sauce.
Simmer for a few minutes until the dish is heated through.

4. Garnish and Serve:

Garnish the Thai Red Curry Noodles with chopped fresh cilantro and Thai basil leaves.
Serve hot with lime wedges on the side.
Enjoy your delicious Thai Red Curry Noodles!

Feel free to customize this recipe by adding your favorite protein, such as shrimp or chicken. Thai Red Curry Noodles offer a perfect blend of spicy, sweet, and savory flavors in a comforting noodle dish.

Beef Bulgogi Udon

Ingredients:

For the Bulgogi Marinade:

- 1 lb thinly sliced beef (ribeye or sirloin)
- 1/2 cup soy sauce
- 3 tablespoons brown sugar
- 2 tablespoons sesame oil
- 1 tablespoon mirin
- 1 tablespoon rice vinegar
- 3 cloves garlic, minced
- 1 tablespoon ginger, grated
- 2 green onions, finely chopped
- 1 teaspoon sesame seeds
- 1/4 teaspoon black pepper

For the Udon Noodles:

- 8 oz udon noodles, cooked according to package instructions
- 1 tablespoon vegetable oil

For Stir-Frying:

- 1 tablespoon vegetable oil
- 1 onion, thinly sliced
- 1 red bell pepper, thinly sliced
- 1 carrot, julienned
- 2 cups fresh spinach
- Sesame seeds and sliced green onions for garnish

Instructions:

1. Marinate the Beef:

In a bowl, combine soy sauce, brown sugar, sesame oil, mirin, rice vinegar, minced garlic, grated ginger, chopped green onions, sesame seeds, and black pepper.

Add thinly sliced beef to the marinade, ensuring each piece is well coated. Marinate for at least 30 minutes, or refrigerate for a few hours for deeper flavor.

2. Cook the Udon Noodles:

Cook udon noodles according to the package instructions. Drain and toss with 1 tablespoon of vegetable oil to prevent sticking.

3. Stir-Fry:

Heat 1 tablespoon of vegetable oil in a large pan or wok over medium-high heat. Add sliced onion, red bell pepper, and julienned carrot. Stir-fry for 3-4 minutes until vegetables are tender-crisp.

Add marinated beef to the pan and stir-fry until the beef is cooked through. Toss in fresh spinach and cook until wilted.

4. Combine Udon Noodles:

Add cooked udon noodles to the pan and mix everything together until well combined.

Cook for an additional 2-3 minutes until the noodles are heated through.

5. Garnish and Serve:

Garnish Beef Bulgogi Udon with sesame seeds and sliced green onions.
Serve hot and enjoy your delicious Beef Bulgogi Udon!

Feel free to adjust the vegetables or add other ingredients like mushrooms or bean sprouts based on your preferences. Beef Bulgogi Udon brings together the bold and savory flavors of Korean bulgogi with the satisfying texture of udon noodles for a delightful meal.

Cold Kimchi Noodles

Ingredients:

For the Kimchi Sauce:

- 1 cup kimchi, finely chopped
- 2 tablespoons gochugaru (Korean red pepper flakes)
- 2 tablespoons soy sauce
- 1 tablespoon sesame oil
- 1 tablespoon rice vinegar
- 1 tablespoon sugar
- 1 teaspoon minced garlic
- 1 teaspoon grated ginger
- 1 teaspoon toasted sesame seeds

For the Noodles:

- 8 oz somen or soba noodles, cooked and cooled according to package instructions
- 1 cucumber, julienned
- 1 carrot, julienned
- 2 boiled eggs, sliced
- 2 green onions, chopped
- Fresh cilantro and toasted sesame seeds for garnish

Instructions:

1. Prepare the Kimchi Sauce:

    In a bowl, combine chopped kimchi, gochugaru, soy sauce, sesame oil, rice vinegar, sugar, minced garlic, grated ginger, and toasted sesame seeds. Mix well. Adjust the spiciness and sweetness according to your taste preferences.

2. Assemble the Cold Kimchi Noodles:

In a large mixing bowl, combine the cooked and cooled noodles with the kimchi sauce. Toss until the noodles are well coated.
Add julienned cucumber and carrot to the noodles. Toss again to incorporate the vegetables.
Divide the cold kimchi noodles among serving plates.

3. Garnish and Serve:

Garnish each plate with sliced boiled eggs, chopped green onions, fresh cilantro, and toasted sesame seeds.
Serve immediately and enjoy your delicious Cold Kimchi Noodles!

Feel free to customize this dish by adding other vegetables or proteins like shredded chicken or tofu. The combination of the spicy and tangy kimchi sauce with cold noodles makes this a perfect dish for a light and refreshing meal, especially in warmer weather.

Japanese Shrimp Tempura Udon

Ingredients:

For the Tempura:

- 12 large shrimp, peeled and deveined
- 1 cup all-purpose flour
- 1 cup ice-cold water
- 1 egg
- Ice cubes

For the Udon Soup:

- 8 oz udon noodles, cooked according to package instructions
- 4 cups dashi broth (or substitute with chicken or vegetable broth)
- 2 tablespoons soy sauce
- 1 tablespoon mirin
- 1 tablespoon sake (optional)
- 1 tablespoon sugar
- Salt to taste

For Garnish:

- Sliced green onions
- Shredded nori (seaweed)
- Radish sprouts (kaiware) or bean sprouts
- Grated daikon radish
- Shichimi togarashi (Japanese seven-spice blend)

Instructions:

1. Prepare the Tempura:

    In a bowl, combine all-purpose flour, ice-cold water, and one beaten egg. Mix until the batter is just combined; it's okay if it's a bit lumpy.
    Place ice cubes in the batter to keep it cold.

Heat vegetable oil in a deep fryer or a large, deep pot to 350°F (175°C).
Dip each shrimp into the tempura batter, coating them evenly.
Carefully place the battered shrimp into the hot oil and fry until golden brown and crispy. Remove and place on a paper towel to drain excess oil.

2. Prepare the Udon Soup:

In a pot, combine dashi broth, soy sauce, mirin, sake (if using), sugar, and salt.
Bring to a simmer over medium heat.
Add cooked udon noodles to the broth and heat through.

3. Assemble the Shrimp Tempura Udon:

Divide the udon noodles and broth among serving bowls.
Place 3 shrimp tempura on top of each bowl.

4. Garnish and Serve:

Garnish the Shrimp Tempura Udon with sliced green onions, shredded nori, radish sprouts, and grated daikon radish.
Sprinkle Shichimi togarashi on top for an extra kick.
Serve hot and enjoy your delicious Japanese Shrimp Tempura Udon!

Feel free to customize the soup by adding other vegetables or ingredients like mushrooms or fish cakes. Shrimp Tempura Udon is a classic Japanese dish that combines the crispiness of tempura with the comfort of udon noodles in a flavorful broth.

Pad Kra Pao

Ingredients:

- 1 lb ground chicken (or thinly sliced chicken breast/thigh)
- 2 tablespoons vegetable oil
- 4 cloves garlic, minced
- 2 bird's eye chili peppers, minced (adjust to taste)
- 1 cup fresh Thai basil leaves
- 1 tablespoon oyster sauce
- 1 tablespoon soy sauce
- 1 teaspoon fish sauce
- 1 teaspoon sugar
- Freshly ground black pepper
- Jasmine rice, for serving
- Fried egg, for serving (optional)

Instructions:

1. Cook Jasmine Rice:

    Cook jasmine rice according to package instructions.

2. Stir-Fry:

    Heat vegetable oil in a wok or large pan over medium-high heat.
    Add minced garlic and bird's eye chili peppers. Stir-fry for about 30 seconds until aromatic.
    Add ground chicken to the wok. Break it apart with a spatula and cook until browned.
    In a small bowl, mix oyster sauce, soy sauce, fish sauce, and sugar. Pour the sauce over the chicken and stir to combine.
    Continue cooking for another 2-3 minutes until the chicken is cooked through and the sauce has coated the meat.

3. Add Basil:

Add fresh Thai basil leaves to the wok. Stir-fry until the basil leaves are wilted and infused with the flavors of the dish.
Season with freshly ground black pepper to taste.

4. Serve:

Serve the Pad Kra Pao over jasmine rice.
Optionally, top with a fried egg.
Enjoy your delicious Pad Kra Pao!

Feel free to adjust the spiciness by adding more or fewer chili peppers according to your taste. Pad Kra Pao is a quick and satisfying Thai dish that delivers bold flavors with the aromatic Thai basil and a perfect balance of sweet, salty, and spicy notes.

Taiwanese Beef Noodle Soup

Ingredients:

For the Beef Marinade:

- 1 lb beef shank or brisket, thinly sliced
- 2 tablespoons soy sauce
- 2 tablespoons Shaoxing wine (Chinese cooking wine)
- 1 tablespoon sesame oil
- 1 tablespoon sugar
- 1 teaspoon five-spice powder

For the Soup Base:

- 2 tablespoons vegetable oil
- 1 large onion, sliced
- 3 cloves garlic, minced
- 1 thumb-sized ginger, sliced
- 2 tablespoons doubanjiang (fermented bean paste)
- 2 tablespoons tomato paste
- 1 tablespoon chili bean sauce (toban djan)
- 8 cups beef or vegetable broth
- 2 tablespoons soy sauce
- 1 tablespoon dark soy sauce
- 1 tablespoon sugar
- 2 star anise
- 1 cinnamon stick
- 3 dried red chilies (optional for extra heat)
- Salt and pepper to taste

For Assembly:

- 1 lb fresh or dried wheat noodles, cooked according to package instructions
- Bok choy or baby bok choy, blanched
- Green onions, chopped
- Fresh cilantro, chopped

- Chili oil (optional)

Instructions:

1. Marinate the Beef:

    In a bowl, combine sliced beef with soy sauce, Shaoxing wine, sesame oil, sugar, and five-spice powder. Let it marinate for at least 30 minutes.

2. Prepare the Soup Base:

    In a large pot or Dutch oven, heat vegetable oil over medium heat.
    Add sliced onions, minced garlic, and sliced ginger. Cook until fragrant.
    Stir in doubanjiang, tomato paste, and chili bean sauce. Cook for 1-2 minutes.
    Add beef broth, soy sauce, dark soy sauce, sugar, star anise, cinnamon stick, and dried red chilies. Bring to a boil and then reduce heat to simmer for about 30 minutes.
    Taste the broth and adjust seasoning with salt and pepper.

3. Cook the Beef:

    In a separate pan, heat a bit of oil over medium-high heat.
    Sear the marinated beef slices until browned on both sides. Add the beef to the simmering broth.
    Continue simmering for an additional 30 minutes or until the beef is tender.

4. Assemble the Taiwanese Beef Noodle Soup:

    Cook the noodles according to package instructions.
    Place a portion of noodles in each serving bowl. Ladle the soup and beef over the noodles.
    Add blanched bok choy on top and garnish with chopped green onions and cilantro.
    Optionally, drizzle with chili oil for extra heat.
    Serve hot and enjoy your delicious Taiwanese Beef Noodle Soup!

Feel free to customize the recipe by adding your favorite vegetables or adjusting the spice level to suit your taste. Taiwanese Beef Noodle Soup is a comforting and satisfying dish that's perfect for any occasion.

Spicy Sesame Cold Noodles

Ingredients:

For the Noodles:

- 8 oz Chinese wheat noodles or egg noodles
- 1 tablespoon sesame oil

For the Sauce:

- 3 tablespoons soy sauce
- 2 tablespoons rice vinegar
- 2 tablespoons tahini (sesame paste)
- 1 tablespoon sesame oil
- 1 tablespoon sugar
- 1 tablespoon chili oil (adjust to taste for spice level)
- 2 cloves garlic, minced
- 1 teaspoon grated ginger

For Garnish:

- Thinly sliced cucumber
- Shredded carrots
- Chopped green onions
- Toasted sesame seeds
- Chopped cilantro

Instructions:

1. Cook the Noodles:

    Cook the Chinese wheat noodles or egg noodles according to the package instructions. Drain and rinse under cold water to stop the cooking process. Toss the cooked noodles with 1 tablespoon of sesame oil to prevent sticking. Set aside.

2. Prepare the Sauce:

> In a bowl, whisk together soy sauce, rice vinegar, tahini, sesame oil, sugar, chili oil, minced garlic, and grated ginger. Adjust the spice level to your liking.

3. Assemble the Spicy Sesame Cold Noodles:

> Pour the prepared sauce over the cooked and cooled noodles.
> Toss the noodles until they are well coated with the sauce.

4. Garnish and Serve:

> Divide the noodles among serving plates.
> Top the noodles with thinly sliced cucumber, shredded carrots, chopped green onions, toasted sesame seeds, and chopped cilantro.
> Optionally, drizzle with extra chili oil for additional spice.
> Serve immediately and enjoy your Spicy Sesame Cold Noodles!

Feel free to customize the dish by adding proteins such as grilled chicken, shrimp, or tofu. Spicy Sesame Cold Noodles are a quick and tasty dish that combines the nuttiness of sesame with a kick of spice for a delightful meal.

www.ingramcontent.com/pod-product-compliance
Lightning Source LLC
LaVergne TN
LVHW061939070526
838199LV00060B/3882